Organizational Romance Policies and Sexual Favoritism in the #MeToo Workplace

Legal, Ethical, and Practical Considerations for Management

Bahaudin G. Mujtaba and **Frank J. Cavico**

ILEAD Academy, LLC
Davie, Florida. United States of America
www.ileadacademy.com

Bahaudin G. Mujtaba and Frank J. Cavico, 2022. *Organizational Romance Policies and Sexual Favoritism in the #MeToo Workplace: Legal, Ethical, and Practical Considerations for Management*

Cover Design by: Cagri Tanyar

ISBN-13: 978-1-936237-21-0

ISBN-10: 1-936237-21-0

Subject Code & Description
    BUS008000 - Business & Economics: Business Ethics
    BUS010000 - Business & Economics: Business Law
    PHI005000   - Philosophy: Ethics & Moral Philosophy

Printed in the United States of America by ILEAD Academy, LLC. Davie, Florida.

Table of Contents

Preface

This book is about workplace relationships, specifically romantic ones, along with the closely related construct, sexual conduct, which can lead to happiness and joy yet also sadness and bitterness, as well as the legal and ethical challenges in situations of sexual harassment. The authors encourage managers and business leaders to become aware and create relevant workplace romance policies that are sustainable, inclusive, and best for the organization, society, and everyone in the world.

Researchers have empirically proven that "Known romantic liaisons[1] can have both positive and negative outcomes, such as increased job involvement, engagement, and work motivation among romance participants, yet at the same time decrease work group morale, especially when a hierarchal romance between a manager or supervisor and a directly reporting subordinate is involved. So, general friendships as well as sexual relationships or other sexual conduct in the workplace, including among professional colleagues, are "realities of life" for all people. And this fact is especially more prevalent today due to the widespread existence of technology and social media. Notably, it has been said that,

> The use of new social media technologies such as Facebook, LinkedIn, and Twitter, as well as Foursquare, internet blogs, and instant text messaging on iPhones, Droids, Blackberrys and other personal communication devices have created situations where some employees complain that another employee may have created a hostile work environment for them outside the office which then impacts their behavior inside the office. In

---

[1] Mainiero and Jones, 2013a, p. 367.

this new day and age of social networking, friending a coworker on Facebook or allowing the release of one's personal cell phone number as a result of a personal romantic relationship may be fine initially but may turn to harassment or stalking behavior once the relationship has ended (Mainiero and Jones, 2013a, p. 368).

As such, in this book, the authors attempt to examine some of the important topics of sexual favoritism and office romance in the workplace from practical, legal, and ethical perspectives. Accordingly, the book addresses the laws regarding sexual favoritism in the workplace for employees, managers, and organizations to benefit from it.

The three main legal areas – the general rule of isolated instances of sexual favoritism, the *quid pro quo* exception, and the hostile environment exception – are explained and illustrated. The legal vs. the moral dichotomy of the general rule of sexual favoritism is underscored.

The book addresses some of the legal aspects of office romance, particularly how office romance can engender sexual favoritism and then cause sexual harassment and discrimination in the workplace. The book analyzes the topics of sexual favoritism and office romance from an ethical perspective to determine the morality of certain workplace policies and conduct. Four ethical theories are applied to make moral conclusions, to wit: Ethical Egoism, Ethical Relativism, Utilitarianism, and Kantian ethics.

The positive vs. negative consequences of office romance are set forth in a balanced manner. Based on the legal and ethical analysis, the authors make several practical recommendations for management, first, generally, to avoid lawsuits for sexual harassment and discrimination and to curtail sexual favoritism, and then specifically regarding appropriate workplace romance policies and procedures, with particular attention on the so-called "love contract," and "non-disclosure agreements" (NDAs) linked to sexual harassment cases.

The goal of this book is to help employers and managers to attain a workplace that is practical, effective, functional, and efficacious, but very importantly also one that is legal, fair, ethical, moral, and just. Workplace relationships are likely to form as a natural consequence of human beings working together and developing strong bonds due to mutual respect and professionalism as well as basic physical attraction. If you find yourself or some of your employees in such a relationship, "no worries," as this book will help you to navigate through it all professionally. In any workplace relationship, think like a lawyer by making sure that how you conduct yourself is legal, fair, ethical, and moral from all perspectives.

As authors, we wish you not "only" organizational success, but also great personal and professional relationships that are joyful, sustainable, and full of mutual love and respect.

Sincerely,
Bahaudin and Frank

Acknowledgements

First, we would like to thank the following colleagues and research assistants for their contributions and guidance in preparing this book:

1) Anjali Samaroo
2) Cagri Tanyar
3) Kaukab Khan
4) Lwendjina (Jina) Estelien
5) Nala Beatrice

The authors in particular want to thank their Huizenga College colleagues and students for their editing suggestions and feedback.

Second, we would like to thank all those who have helped us get to this point.

Third, we thank you for reading this material. For suggestions and questions, you can contact us by email (cavico@nova.edu or mujtaba@nova.edu) at any time.

Introduction

The advent of the #MeToo movement has brought forth increased national attention to sexual assault, abuse, misconduct, discrimination, and harassment in the workplace, especially by prominent men against subordinate female employees. The seriousness of the situation is evidenced by research polls, to wit, one a Pew research poll, which reported that 42% of women surveyed believe they have experienced some form of sex discrimination at work, and an NPR/PBS poll which revealed that 35% of women in the U.S. have experienced sexual harassment in the workplace[2]. As such, important objectives of the movement are to encourage women to come forward and disclose sexual discrimination and harassment and to promote equality, dignity, respect, and civility in the workplace. Many of the high-profile sexual cases that generated the #MeToo movement involved powerful male executives asserting that their romantic relationships with subordinate females in the workplace were "merely" consensual office romance and sexual favoritism.

One famous example involves the President of CNN, Jeff Zucker, who resigned in February 2022 stating that his

---

[2] Kreis, 2020, p. 149

romantic relationship with another female executive had become progressively more serious over the years. He stated that he was required to disclose the romantic relationship when it began as per the company policy, but he did not. So, Mr. Zucker took personal responsibility for not disclosing the romantic relationship and chose to resign. Similarly, in another high-profile case, McDonald's former Chief Executive Officer (CEO), Steve Easterbrook, voluntarily terminated his position with the company in 2019 after he was voted out by the company's board of directors for becoming involved in a relationship with an employee. Easterbrook did agree that he made a mistake while acknowledging McDonald's company values. Easterbrook's workplace romance violated McDonald's policy against conflicts of interest. While it cannot be clear if such high-profile workplace romantic relationships are always due to respect or honest attraction between two consenting adults, such relationships can lead to cases of sexual harassment, and even a lawsuit for *quid pro quo* or *hostile working environment*, particularly if a powerful person is involved. Initially, it should be emphasized that any form of unwelcome sexual advances and/or requests for sexual favors by managers as a condition of employment decisions are actionable under Title VII of the Civil Rights Act of 1964.

Another example of workplace romantic relationship is when the CIA Director David H. Petraeus resigned due to having an extramarital affair with Paula Broadwell, who was a former military officer and the co-author of a biography about General Petraeus. While most workplace romances become news due to gossip, General Petraeus's affair was discovered and made public as part of an FBI investigation into a potential security breach involving his e-mails. Of course, there are many other local and national examples of celebrities, respected professionals, and local colleagues related to workplace romance which can lead to organizational concerns related to favoritism, sexual harassment, and retaliation.

Ultimately, due to the serious nature of these incidents and the visibility of high-profile cases, some fear workplace romance, while others do not see anything new other than the need for more awareness. The following statements summarize the views and comments coming from some males and females:

- *"As a woman, I don't see anything new from the #MeToo movement, other than more coverage, as I was fully aware of abuses facing women."*
- *"As a man, I am afraid to make the first move and ask a female colleague on a date."*

It is perfectly clear that all men and women would want a healthy work environment for everyone along with "some" clarity regarding workplace romance policies, whether predicated on friendship, intimacy, or social, professional, and/or acquaintance relationships. As demonstrated by research (Figure 1) from Vault Careers (2018), some firms (surprisingly 20%) do not have any policies regarding workplace romantic relationships, while most organizations do provide certain guidance and directions on how to handle such socializations, engagements, and involvements. While only 2% of the firms forbid all workplace romances, almost all firms that have a policy would not approve of supervisor-employee romantic involvements. Colleagues that do get romantically involved, moreover, are often required to report the relationship immediately to their managers and human resource department, which can lead to one of the employees being transferred to another department or retirement.

DOES YOUR COMPANY HAVE A POLICY
REGARDING OFFICE ROMANCES?

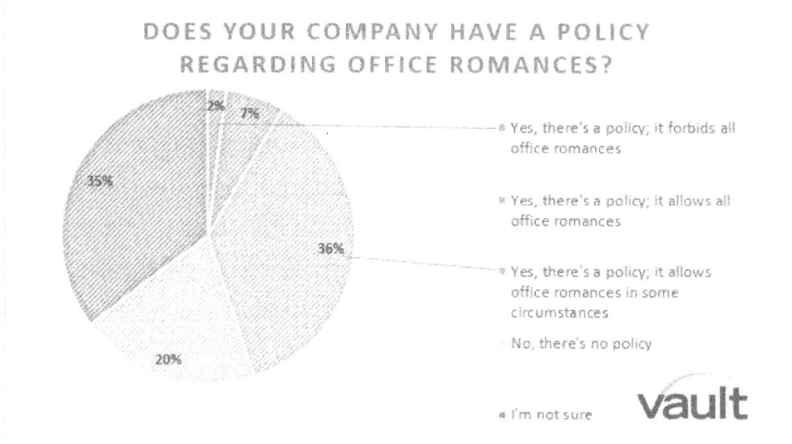

Figure 1 – Policies of Workplace Romance
(Source: Vault Careers, February 11, 2018)

Vault Career's office romance survey included 654 responses from working professionals with 62% from men, and 38% from women working in such fields as education, law, healthcare, marketing, consulting, etc. It showed that about 52% of these professionals have had at least one office romance (Figure 2), and 78% of them are open to being in such a relationship again – which probably means that most of the other 22% are happily married because of their workplace connection. One popular and successful example is the fact that the former President Barack H. Obama met his wife Michelle Obama at the workplace when they were both practicing law. Workplace relationships are a reality of life between consenting adults, who become attracted to each other due to respect, love, similarities, professional goals, and other such ideals. Mainiero and Jones (2013a) mentioned that 64% of those who had a workplace romantic relationship would certainly get involved once again if the opportunity presented itself.

According to Elsesser (2019), while it was predicted that the #MeToo movement would discourage employees from dating co-workers, the statistics showed the opposite. In almost three in four, 72%, would participate in an office romance. As these statistics demonstrate that romantic relationship will be the norm in the workplace, employers and organizations should be aware to guide these growing pairs through the process to reduce risks of hostility, gossip, lawsuits, and to create a safer environment for all. The data clearly shows that employees need relevant policies since workplace romance relationships are going to be a reality, and consequently employers need to make sure they provide clear directions.

For a small number of organizations, signing a "love contract" becomes mandatory for those who get romantically involved. The "love contracts" usually ensure that the relationship is consensual and not a case of *quid-pro-quo*; and it has language to avoid all forms of favoritism or conflicts of interest, and also a clear statement that there will not be any legal consequences against the company if the relationship comes to an end. Overall, "A love contract[3] specifies that the employer desires to avoid misunderstandings, actual or potential conflicts of interest, complaints of favoritism, possible claims of sexual harassment, and employee morale and dissension problems that can potentially result from romantic relationships. If used, such contracts should specify, according to the firm's ethical code of conduct, appropriate versus inappropriate social media contacts and consequences."

Sexual favoritism in a workplace romantic relationship can be when an employee who is in a subordinate position receives special treatment, unearned salary increases, or even

---

[3] Mainiero and Jones, 2013a, p. 377.

promotions due to a sexual affiliation with another colleague who is in a position of power or higher rank. There are lateral and hierarchical workplace romances[4]. *Lateral* workplace romance is when a romantic relationship brews between two employees of the same status or rank and power. *Hierarchical* workplace romance is when the involved employees are on different organizational rankings or levels of authority based on their positions. The latter, hierarchical, is more challenging as it can lead to more cases of favoritism and hostility in the workplace. Even though sexual favoritism does not directly violate any laws related to the Title VII or civil rights acts, it can indirectly create a hostile work environment and lead to favoritism. Since favoritism can lead to *quid pro quo*, it can create a perception that managers would only promote employees who engage in sexual relationships with them.

Some companies have had the "*forced arbitration*" clause for their employees who experience discrimination, pay inequity, or sexual harassment, but the U.S. Senate passed legislation on February 10, 2022, that would end forced arbitration in cases of sexual assault and harassment. This means that organizations cannot force employees to settle their sexual assault or harassment cases in private or secretly. As such, employees that did sign the "forced arbitration" clause can take their case into public courts to sue their employers, rather than going into arbitration. The "forced arbitration" clauses had generally deprived employees of being able to go to court when a company or manager violates the law, because it required the victims to settle the case secretly, which usually favors the company. Whatever the policies are at any organization, Mainiero and Jones (2013a, p. 367) recommend that human resource professionals take an active role in

---

[4] Yuldashev and and Yusupov, 2016.

communicating the proper ethical rules regarding romantic workplace relationships and conducts.

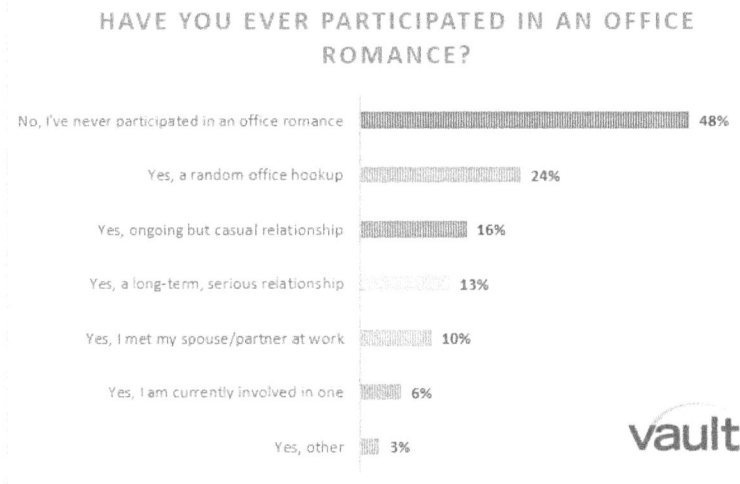

HAVE YOU EVER PARTICIPATED IN AN OFFICE ROMANCE?

No, I've never participated in an office romance	48%
Yes, a random office hookup	24%
Yes, ongoing but casual relationship	16%
Yes, a long-term, serious relationship	13%
Yes, I met my spouse/partner at work	10%
Yes, I am currently involved in one	6%
Yes, other	3%

vault

Figure 2 – Workplace Romance Participation
(Source: Vault Careers, February 11, 2018)

As a result of the #MeToo movement and high profile lawsuits (such as the film producer Harvey Weinstein, Matt Lauer of NBC News, Roger Ailes of FOX television, former President Bill Clinton's affair with White House intern Monica Lewinsky, Justice Clarence Thomas being accused of sexual harassment by Anita Hill, the Self-Help guru Tony Robbins being accused of inappropriate sexual advances, Justice Brett Kavanaugh being accused of sexual assault by professor Christine Blasey Ford, the chief executive of CBS Corporation Les Moonves being accused of sexual harassment and assault by six women, actor Kevin Spacey being accused of sexual misconduct by co-workers, actor Steven Seagal being accused of sexual harassment and assault by multiple women, Charlie Rose of PBS being accused of crude sexual advances by eight female colleagues, Travis Smiley of PBS engaging in sexual relationships with multiple subordinates, etc.), employers have been compelled to reconsider how they should respond to sexual discrimination, sexual harassment, office romance, and sexual favoritism in the workplace.

Sometimes what the person in the position of authority is doing is not necessarily illegal, but it can be unethical as it makes victims and those watching feel uncomfortable in the work environment. Therefore, "When office decorum[5] is disrupted by a failed office romance, we believe it becomes the firm's responsibility to act to protect the employee who no longer desires the office romance and also the co-workers who inadvertently have become part of the office romance drama."

Accordingly, a principal aim of this book is to analyze one important aspect of office romance and sexual conduct in the workplace, to wit: the practice of sexual favoritism, which is also called "paramour favoritism" or "paramour preference." The practice of sexual favoritism will be analyzed from legal, ethical, and practical perspectives. The book will also provide recommendations to management on how to avoid liability for sexual harassment pursuant to Title VII of the Civil Rights Act. The book, moreover, seeks to examine sexual favoritism and sexual harassment in the broader context of "office romance" in the era of the #MeToo movement. Office romance, of course, can result in sexual relationships which can cause sexual favoritism in the workplace, which then can lead to lawsuits for sexual discrimination and harassment. The authors will analyze workplace romances and make recommendations as to fair, just,

---

[5] Mainiero and Jones, 2013a, p. 369.

and practical office romance policies, especially policies that will avoid sexual harassment and favoritism.

An additional and important objective of this book is to examine another prevalent business practice related to the topics addressed herein, and one which also has been significantly affected by the #MeToo movement – the use of non-disclosure agreements (NDAs) in sexual harassment lawsuits. Accordingly, the authors will define NDAs and explain their principal components, discuss their use in sexual harassment cases, analyze the legality and morality of NDAs, and provide appropriate recommendations to employers and managers as to NDA use in sexual harassment cases. Of course, anywhere human beings interact with each other and are exposed to different colleagues can bring about situations of attraction, romance, and fraternization which can at times lead to legal concerns.

Impact and Exposure

Over five decades ago, Robert B. Zajonc (1968) hypothesized whether repeated exposure of an individual to a stimulus object enhances their attitude towards the stimulus. To test this hypothesis, participants were shown pictures of different men from a yearbook, some men were shown more frequently and others less. The study found that the men who were shown more frequently had higher favorability of attitude among the study participants.

In another experiment, the hypothesis was tested using repeated exposures of nonsense words three times due to experimental errors. Two words appeared 25 times, two 10 times, two 5 times, two twice, and two once. The position of a word in the series of trials was determined by a random device.

The third trial of the study shows that as the frequency of exposure increases there is a higher sense of familiarity and possibly comfort with whatever is being seen. Empirical studies[6] have demonstrated that where continuous reinforcement have been used, the individual's frequency of exposure correlated with a positive attitude. Despite the findings being in favor of a positive correlation with exposure and favorability of attitude, it is hard to say with confidence that the hypothesis is one hundred percent correct. On a theoretical level, the questions and results are considered psychological processes that mediate exposure effects.

The results of empirical studies provide a solid indication that prolonged exposure to a stimulus can affect attraction or attitudinal liking towards the stimulus. If we apply the results to workplace romance, we can explain the increase in the percentage of those who have engaged in workplace romance and fraternization. Anecdotally, we can see that exposure around coworkers can increase attraction towards one another. The *"mere exposure effect"* is said to be a psychological phenomenon where people tend to develop a preference for things or people who are more familiar with them. In times of great challenge or even excitement, people tend to go to those they are most familiar with and trust.

Examples of exposure and detailed fraternization can be seen from the Army and healthcare industry. The policies of such industries are interesting because in these professions workers are at work for extended periods of time and often enough do not have time outside of their work. This means their dating pool is limited to those they meet at work and become familiar with due to repeated exposures.

---

[6] Premack, 1965.

Workplace romance can increase happiness of employees who are in legitimate and successful relationships. However, workplace relationships can also have a negative impact on the work environment. For example, gossip and complaints result in employees being demotivated and feelings of sexual favoritism.

Employees that engage in sexual favoritism and workplace romance can end up in challenging dilemmas. For example, poor communication among employees, not sharing relevant information due to avoiding contact with one's colleague, as well as avoiding some groups due to a romantic relationship with a colleague, can all be hurtful to the department and organization. Some employees voluntarily choose to transfer to work with other departments or companies to avoid meeting a former romantically involved colleague. Therefore, romantic relationships can have a destructive impact on productivity and can also demotivate other employees that are observing the relationship.

Workplace romances, moreover, do often result in gossiping among employees, suppliers, and customers, which can generate feelings of sexual favors by managers and leaders. Real and perceived feelings of sexual favoritism can decrease collegiality and respect among employees. During the beginning stages of dating encounters, there may not be a need to disclose a relationship with the other colleague as you are simply "getting to know" the other person. When dating persists over time and slowly transitions into a romantic relationship, then it is often required and mandatory[7] to disclose the relationship to avoid gossip and feelings of favoritism. It is important that those who are romantically involved keep their

---

[7] Chory and Hoke, 2019

relationship issues out of the working environment and focus on their jobs and the company's productivity. It is also imperative to note that when a manager is dating a subordinate employee, then such a problematical situation usually requires that one of the parties' transfers, quits, or retires.

Some organizations allow workplace romance, while others strictly prohibit it. While firms cannot stop romantic relationships, they can regulate its negative impact. Overall, a workplace environment should be comprised of professional relationships to avoid the negative impacts associated with gossip, sexual favoritism and lawsuits related to assault, harassment, discrimination, and a hostile work environment.

Harassment and Discrimination

Title VII prohibits discrimination based on sex in all the terms and conditions of employment. Sexual harassment, moreover, has been construed by the U.S. Supreme Court in the seminal *Meritor Savings Bank v. Vinson* (1986) case to be equivalent of illegal sexual discrimination pursuant to Title VII. Furthermore, illegal sexual harassment can consist of two types of conduct: first, *quid pro quo*, which is decision-making in the workplace based on the submission to or rejection of unwelcome sexual conduct; and second, unwelcome and repeated sexual conduct that unreasonably interferes with a person's job performance or which creates an abusive, intimidating, offensive, and/or hostile[8] work environment. Moreover, the Supreme Court has considerably broadened the exposure of employers for sexual harassment committed by their employees. If there is sexual harassment inflicted by a manager or supervisor to a

---

[8] EEOC, *Policy Guidance*, 1990

subordinate employee in the management hierarchy, and the employee suffers a tangible job loss, such as being discharged or even just losing time from work due to stress, then the employer is absolutely liable for the sexual harassment. There is no defense. Absolute means absolute. The only "solution" in such a scenario is sexual harassment insurance.

Employers today, therefore, should be especially sensitive to office romance due to the potential of workplace sexual discrimination and sexual harassment claims, particularly since the U.S. Supreme Court has ruled that an employer may be absolutely liable for the sexual harassment of an executive, manager, or supervisor who sexually harasses a subordinate employee in the managerial hierarchical chain. Sexual harassment is premised on a workplace environment that is hostile, offensive, or abusive sexually. The legal standard for what constitutes a hostile sexual environment is a very subjective one too. Employees can sue an employer for allowing a hostile sexual environment to occur and also for not stopping the offensive sexual behavior. The problem for the employer is exacerbated when the relationship was originally consensual but now one party wants to break it off, but the other party still persists in making unwelcome romantic advances. Furthermore, even though the federal civil rights act does not protect against discrimination based on marital status, about two dozen states and many municipalities have laws that ban discrimination on the basis of marriage. A legal problem in such a state or city might arise if a married employee who has an affair is terminated, but an unmarried employee who has an affair is not discharged. The married employee could well claim illegal discrimination based on his or her marital status. Another legal problem for employers is that employees are entitled to privacy rights – pursuant to constitutional law for government employees, but also pursuant to tort law for all employees. An employer who too intrusively investigates its employees' romantic relationships or discharges employees for such relationships may be sued for intentionally violating[9] the employees' privacy rights. So, clearly, there are many legal aspects to office romance.

This book in the Legal section first addresses the laws regarding sexual favoritism in the workplace. The three main legal areas – the general rule of isolated instances of sexual favoritism, the *quid pro quo* exception, and the hostile environment exception – are explained and illustrated in the context of sexual favoritism. The book then addresses some of the legal aspects of office romance, particularly in relationship to sexual favoritism in the workplace. Next, we analyze the topics of sexual favoritism and office romance from ethical perspectives to determine the morality of certain workplace policies and conduct. Four ethical theories are applied to make moral conclusions, to wit: Ethical Egoism, Ethical Relativism, Utilitarianism, and Kantian ethics. Then, based on the legal and ethical analysis, the authors make recommendations for management, first, generally, to avoid lawsuits for sexual harassment and discrimination and to curtail sexual favoritism, and then specifically regarding appropriate office romance policies and procedures. We conclude the book by a discussion of values and business leadership in the context of sexual favoritism and office romance. The goal is to help employers and managers to achieve a practical, functional, and efficacious workplace, and one that is legal, fair, ethical, and just.

---

[9] Cavico and Mujtaba, 2021; Cavico and Mujtaba, 2014; Cavico, Mujtaba, and Samuels, 2012.

Legal Analysis

The principal purpose of this legal section is to explain to management the extent to which the employer can be held liable for discriminating against otherwise qualified job applicants and employees by denying them employment, advancement, opportunity, or benefit in the workplace because the person who received the position, opportunity, or benefit received it because he or she submitted to unwelcome *or* welcome sexual advances or requests. Although the focus is on federal law, specifically Title VII of the Civil Rights Act and EEOC policy statements, guidelines, and examples, reference to pertinent state civil rights laws is also made. The general rule regarding sexual favoritism in the workplace and the two exceptions – *quid pro quo* harassment and hostile environment harassment are explained and illustrated in the context of sexual favoritism.

Instances of Sexual Favoritism

The general legal rule is that sexual favoritism does not violate Title VII if the conduct consists of isolated instances of preferential treatment based on consensual office romance relationships. The rationale is that granting a preference to a paramour based on the consensual romantic relationship does not amount to discrimination against women or men since both are equally disadvantaged[10] for reasons other than their gender. The Equal Employment Opportunity Commission (EEOC) further explains the rationale: "A female charging party who is

---

[10] see, for example, *Doyle v. Advanced Fraud Sols., LLC*, 2020; *Romero v. McCormick & Schmick Rest. Corp.*, 2020; *Kieffer v. Tractor Supply Co.*, 2019; *Miller v. Aluminum Co. of America*, 1988; *DeCinto v. Westchester County Medical Center*, 1986; *Blount v. Northrop Grumman Info. Tech Overseas, Inc.*, 2014, applying Virginia law; EEOC, *Policy Guidance*, 1990.

denied an employment benefit because of such sexual favoritism would not have been treated more favorably had she been a man, nor, conversely, was she treated less favorably because she was a woman" (EEOC, *Policy Guidance*, 1990, p. 3.) That is, Title VII is not triggered because the preferential treatment is based on the sexual conduct of the parties rather than the gender[11] of the employees.

However, from a legalistic perspective it should be noted that technically the EEOC's precepts are not conventional administrative rules and regulations, but "merely guidelines" for employers. However, the authors would emphasize that the EEOC is more than willing to sue an employer for contravening its "guidelines," thus forcing the employer to litigate in the courts, where a federal court may agree or disagree with the agency's guidelines. Moreover, Byun (2014) underscores that the guidelines have been "influential" in the decision-making of the courts (p. 269). Kreis (2020) also notes that the general rule of no liability "principle is derived from decades of precedent holding that paramour discrimination and sexual favoritism are generally not actionable under Title VII" (p. 191). Kreis (2020) further explains that these "paramour cases are not actionable because they are not structural or systemic sex-based roadblocks to equal workforce opportunity" (p. 192). Moreover, even though Title VII prohibits retaliatory discrimination, since office romance as well as discrimination based on consensual sexual relationships are neither protected nor prohibited by Title VII, opposition to such relationships is also not protected as illegal[12] retaliation.

---

[11] see the following cases which are in conformity with the EEOC rule and rationales: *Doyle v. Advanced Fraud Sols., LLC*, 2020; *Kieffer v. Tractor Supply Co.*, 2019.
[12] *Poff v. Oklahoma*, 2017.

Consequently, there are many recent cases where the courts have ruled that the sexual favoritism or paramour preference is "merely" isolated, and thus there is no legal liability. The authors will now illustrate a few recent cases. First, in the federal district court case of *Doyle v. Advanced Fraud Sols., LLC* (2020), the company's president, a male, began a consensual affair with a female subordinate employee, had her transferred to his location, and allegedly provided her with favorable treatment compared to other employees, for example, allowing her to work from home while other employees were not, as well as providing her with "inappropriate" benefits, such as meals and hotel rooms, at the company's expense, which latter benefits the plaintiff, a female and the company's marketing coordinator, claimed was a "misuse" of company funds. There was, however, no evidence presented that the president and his paramour engaged in any "sexual banter" at work or that he made any inappropriate sexual remarks. Accordingly, the court dismissed the Title VII claim, saying that this situation was just a case of legally permissible sexual preference and that there was no illegal discrimination because both males and females in the workplace were denied the benefits the president granted to his paramour[13].

In the federal district court case of *McKissic v. City of Reno* (2019), the city manager, a male, was allegedly having a romantic affair with an assistant city manager, a female, to whom he granted a favorable assignment; and he also allegedly failed to hold her accountable for work-related mistakes. Another assistant city manager sued, claiming the sexual favoritism violated Title VII. The court however, disagreed,

---

[13] *Doyle v. Advanced Fraud Sols., LLC*, 2020.

explaining that the "alleged favoritism…, even accepted as true, does not meet the requisite barometer of ubiquity[14] to support a Title VII claim." The court did note that there was hostility directed to the plaintiff by the city manager but that the hostility was not sexual in nature but as a result of perceived incompetent work performance by the plaintiff and "team problems" with her work team[15]. Similarly, in the federal district court case of *Stewart v. SBE Entm't Grp., LLC* (2017), the plaintiffs, cocktail waitresses, contended they were treated illegally by the company due to sexual favoritism because certain supervisors who were dating other cocktail waitresses exempted their paramours from the company's policy of no-alcohol consumption at work, while strictly enforcing the policy, including the use of breathalyzer tests, on the plaintiff cocktail waitresses. Yet there was no evidence of any unwanted sexual advances – physical or otherwise - by management. The court thus deemed this "favoritism" conduct to be consensual, preferential, but isolated and not "ubiquitous," and thus the court ruled that the conduct "without more cannot support a sex-discrimination claim under Title VII" (*Stewart v. SBE Entm't Grp., LLC*, 2017, p. 1244).

Another example is the federal district court case of *Binion V. PNC Bank, Nat'l Ass'n* (2017), where the plaintiff, a female bank customer representative, contended she was discriminated against when the branch manager, a male, hired another female as a customer service representative with whom he was allegedly having a romantic affair. The plaintiff alleged that his paramour was given favorable treatment in the form of bank business being funneled to her, being unfairly given credit

---

[14] *McKissic v. City of Reno*, 2019, p. 22
[15] *McKissic v. City of Reno*, 2019.

for successful work, allowing her to take long lunches, and that she would stay in his office and sit on top of his desk. The plaintiff asserted, moreover, that in order to take care of his paramour and to protect her, the branch manager got the plaintiff transferred and ultimately worked to getting her fired (for violating the bank's code of ethics). The court, however, ruled against her on the discrimination claim, explaining that Title VII does not encompass a discrimination claim based on isolated favoritism to a supervisor's paramour; and, moreover, the court explained that such a romantic relationship is "akin to nepotism." Even favoritism based on "friendship" where the parties are not dating is not actionable, stated the court. Furthermore, even if sexual favoritism played a role in the manager's getting the plaintiff transferred and ultimately fired, there still would be no liability under Title VII. There also was no evidence of unwelcome sexual conduct directed to the plaintiff and no evidence that the manager's sexual conduct permeated the workplace; and thus, the plaintiff's discrimination claim was dismissed on summary judgement by the court[16].

A final example of isolated sexual favoritism is the federal district court case of *Crisanto v. Cnty. Tulare* (2015), where the plaintiff, a female, and a lead psychologist for a government agency, contended that her immediate supervisor discriminated against her by favoring another female employee, his wife. Specifically, the plaintiff complained that her supervisor allowed his wife to routinely escape job discipline for her work indiscretions that would cause discipline for other employees who were not engaged in a marital, romantic, or sexual relationship. Moreover, the plaintiff alleged that her

---

[16] *Binion V. PNC Bank, Nat'l Ass'n*, 2017.

supervisor gave preferential treatment to his wife regarding job compensation, assignments, and benefits. However, the court ruled that there were insufficient facts to show that the supervisor by his preferential treatment of his wife "sexualized" the workplace. There may have been sexual favoritism, but it was neither severe nor pervasive and thus did not alter the conditions in the workplace; rather, here, the favoritism was just directed to one person, the supervisor's wife; and there was no evidence as to any sexual conduct being directed to the plaintiff or any other employees; and, moreover, there was no evidence of any inappropriate touching or displays of affection in the workplace. Accordingly, there was neither a pattern of bias based on sexual availability nor one that was widespread enough to rise to the level of hostile work environment based on sexual conduct; and thus, the plaintiff's lawsuit was dismissed[17].

The preceding cases well illustrated the legal general rule; however, as noted, there are two important exceptions (*quid pro quo* and hostile work environment) which will be covered in the next section.

---

[17] *Crisanto v. Cnty. Tulare*, 2015.

2

Sexual Favoritism and Harassment

In this chapter, we will talk about sexual favoritism related to coercion (*quid pro quo*) and the creation of a hostile work environment for employees in the workplace.

Coerced Sexual Conduct

An important exception to the general rule of no liability for sexual favoritism arises when an employee is coerced into submitting to unwelcome sexual advances in return for a position, promotion, or other job benefit; the submission aspect of the relationship renders the conduct unlawful and thus a cause of action exists not only for the victimized employee but for other employees who were qualified but were denied the employment opportunity or benefit[18]. In such a case, other employees who were qualified but were denied the job benefit may be able to demonstrate that sex was generally made as a condition for receiving the job benefit. That is, according to the

---

[18] *Doyle v. Advanced Fraud Sols., LLC*, 2020 *Stewart v. SBE Entm't Grp., LLC*, 2017.

EEOC, a woman would need to establish that in order to obtain the job benefit, it would have been necessary to grant sexual favors, which is a condition that would not have been imposed on men[19]. The EEOC views the aforementioned situation as constituting a traditional case of *quid pro quo* (sex-for-job; "this-for-that") sexual harassment. The EEOC further explains that even if a manager or supervisor was interested in just one female, and thus coerced only her, other women, as well as men, who were denied the benefit would be able to claim legally impermissible discrimination because they were harmed as a result of the sexual harassment inflicted on the woman who was coerced[20]. The EEOC provides an example of a "coercion" case, to wit: A female employee contends she lost a promotion for which she was qualified because another woman, a co-worker, who obtained the promotion was engaged in a sexual relationship with their supervisor. However, the sexual relationship was not consensual; rather, the supervisor regularly harassed the co-worker, demanded sex as a condition for the promotion, and then he audibly boasted about his "conquest." In such a situation, the EEOC maintains that the female employee who lost the promotion may be able to establish a Title VII violation by demonstrating that in order to obtain the promotion, it would have been necessary for her to grant sexual favors. Moreover, the EEOC submits that in addition she and other qualified male and female co-workers would have legal "standing" to challenge the favoritism on the basis that they were harmed because of the discrimination against the female co-worker who did not get the promotion[21].

---

[19] EEOC, *Policy Guidance*, 1990.
[20] EEOC, *Policy Guidance*, 1990.
[21] EEOC, *Policy Statement*, 1990.

Consent versus coercion are the key elements to this exception. Yet, legally as well as morally, one of the key questions that has been raised as a result of the #MeToo movement, according to Green (2019), is: "What does consent to a romantic relationship mean today with evolving notions inspired by the overwhelming avalanche of misdeeds being identified through the #MeToo movement?" (p. 117). Accordingly, an intriguing situation arises in a case of supposed consensual sex between a manager or supervisor and a subordinate employee, especially if the former is male and the latter is a female. Are such hierarchical workplace romances truly voluntary and consensual? Byun (2014) asserts that due to the "power dynamic" involved in a superior-subordinate relationship in the workplace, these "hierarchical workplace romances can be more troublesome and threatening than lateral romances" (p. 274). As such, Byun (2014) explains that "employees will experience subtle pressure to participate or at least acquiesce to such behavior, whether they like it or not, when the pressure is coming from the boss. This is more troublesome for women who work in a male-dominated environment" (pp. 274-75). Leong (2019) calls the preceding hierarchical relationship one of "institutional power disparity" where the supervisor can control the subordinate's "fates and circumstances as a result of their respective institutional roles" (p. 946). Therefore, Srinivasan (2020) contends that such a "power imbalance" vitiates legal consent; that is, consent is lacking "where a subordinate feels compelled to relent to a supervisor's advances because she fears the consequences of not doing so, even if there is no explicit threat made" (p. 1118). Even if such "consent" means the sex was voluntary in the sense that the female employee did not engage in sex against her will, thereby preventing a *quid pro quo* lawsuit, the implicit coercion and the concomitant implied *quid pro quo* threat perpetuates gender inequality[22]. Furthermore, in situations of "serious power imbalance", such as between supervisor and employee or professor and student, Srinivasan (2020) asserts that the consent might be "subtly coerced", even without the party's knowing (p. 1138). Consequently, some warn that if the potential relationship is between an executive at a high-level in the corporate hierarchy, the "power differentials are too insurmountable"[23].

Therefore, "in light of the power differentials and the public exposure via #MeToo, it is always prudent[24] for employers to establish policies that encourage an executive to refuse to even take the risk of making an overture to see if there can be a consensual relationship with a subordinate". Houseman (2019), in addition, reports on studies that show that if there is a gender imbalance at work, that is, for example, the executives are mainly male and the administrative assistants mainly female, then sexual harassment may occur at a higher rate (p. 287). Actual or perceived retaliation is another means to vitiate consent. Green (2019) explains that: "In considering the harm from potential retaliatory blackballing, subordinates who choose to respond to executives' overtures in ways that limit the potential for retaliation are not really consenting. Those limited subordinate responses, however, could lead executives to believe that the subordinate has consented" (p. 128). Green (2019) adds that "while it may be that a response of 'no means no' in terms of the romantic or sexual encounter,

---

[22] Srinivasan, 2020, pp. 1111, 1114.
[23] Green, 2019, p. 159.
[24] Green, 2019, p. 159.

the subordinate can never be certain that a no does not also mean tremendously adverse career consequences" (p. 163). While the *quid pro quo* exception deals primarily with the relationship of the respective parties, another exception (hostile work environment) arises if the sexual relationships and concomitant sexual favoritism at work are widespread.

The Hostile Sexual Environment

Another important legal exception occurs when office romance and sexual favoritism in the workplace create a hostile work environment, which as noted is a form of sexual harassment. Consequently, if favoritism based on the granting of sexual favors is viewed as widespread in the workplace, female employees, as well as male employees, who do not welcome such conduct can sue on a hostile environment sexual harassment theory, regardless of whether any of the objectionable sexual conduct is directed at them and regardless of whether the sexual favors granted were voluntary and consensual[25]. In such a situation, according to the EEOC[26], "a message is conveyed that the managers view women as 'sexual playthings,' thereby creating an atmosphere that is demeaning to women." Moreover, both men and women can sue pursuant to the hostile environment as well as under the *quid pro quo* doctrine if they find such sexual conduct offensive and it is sufficiently severe and pervasive so as to create an abusive

---

[25] EEOC, *Policy Statement*, 1990; *Wasche v. Orchard Hosp*, 2020; *Stewart v. SBE Entm't Grp., LLC*, 2017; *Cofer v. Parker-Hannifin Corp.*, 2016, applying California law; *Miller v. Dep't of Corr.*, 2005, applying California law; *Broderick v. Ruder*, 1988; Leong, 2019; Cavico, Mujtaba, Petrescu, and Muffler, 2015.
[26] EEOC, *Policy Statement*, 1990, p. 4.

working environment[27]. Pearce and Lipin (2015) further explain the hostile work environment rationale:

> An employer's sexual favoritism or preferential treatment may create a hostile work environment when romantic conduct occurs in an indiscreet manner, causing plaintiffs to believe that favorable treatment may be obtained from the employer in exchange for a sexual or romantic relationship. Co-workers of an employee engaged in such a relationship with a superior may perceive that the person in power favors that employee, thus raising the inference of the existence of the hostile work environment. Under third-party sexual harassment doctrine, this occurs when a supervisor in such a relationship awards benefits to the employee with whom he or she is having a sexual relationship, thereby denying the benefits to similarly situated third-party employees (pp. 322-33).

In determining whether a work environment is "hostile" the EEOC uses a *"totality of the circumstances"* test, whereby on a case-by-case basis using an objective standard of the hypothetical "reasonable person" in the context in which the alleged conduct occurred. Certain factors that the EEOC says should be considered are as follows: the number of incidents of favoritism, the egregiousness of the conduct, and whether other employees in the workplace were aware of the conduct[28]. Similarly, one federal district court advised to consider the

---

[27] EEOC, *Policy Statement*, 1990.
[28] EEOC, *Policy Statement*, 1990.

"totality of the circumstances" and not to consider the allegations "piecemeal"[29]. However, another federal district court also warned that "Title VII is not a 'general civility code,'" and thus "to establish a violation the environment must be both objectively and subjectively abusive."[30] Accordingly, the court explained that plaintiffs need to "offer evidence[31] to show that they were subjected to unwelcome verbal or physical sexual advances by management and that they knew about it."

The following federal cases illustrate the preceding hostile environment rules. First, in the federal district court case of *Broderick v. Ruder* (1988), the court ruled that widespread sexual favoritism can rise to the level of a Title VII sexual harassment violation. In the case, a staff attorney at a federal government agency alleged that two of her supervisors had engaged in sexual relationships with two secretaries who then received promotions, cash rewards, and other job benefits. Moreover, another of her supervisors, a male, allegedly promoted another staff attorney, a female, who he socialized with extensively and to whom the supervisor was noticeably attracted to. Furthermore, there were isolated incidents of sexual harassment directed at the plaintiff herself, including one incident where her supervisor became intoxicated at an office party, untied the plaintiff's sweater, and kissed her[32]. The court found that this conduct created a hostile work environment which was offensive not only to the plaintiff but to other employees at the workplace. In addition, the court found that the supervisor's granting of preferential treatment to those who submitted to his sexual advances undermined the plaintiff's

---

[29] *Garvin v. Southwestern Corr., LLC*, 2019, p. 650.
[30] *Stewart v. SBE Entm't Grp., LLC*, 2017, p. 1245.
[31] *Stewart v. SBE Entm't Grp., LLC*, 2017, p. 1245
[32] *Broderick v. Ruder*, 1988.

motivation to work and thus impaired her job performance, thereby depriving her and other female employees of promotions and other job opportunities. Finally, it is important to note that the EEOC in relating this preceding case in its policy statement stated that "it is the Commission's position that these facts could also support an implicit 'quid pro quo' harassment claim since the managers, by their conduct, communicated a message to all female employees in the office that job benefits would be awarded to those who participated in sexual conduct"[33].

Similarly, in the federal district court case of *Nichol v. City of Springfield* (2017), the plaintiff, a police communications officer for the city, who was terminated, introduced evidence that she reported three different individuals for sexual favoritism. She reported that the former police chief had engaged in a workplace affair, granted favors to his paramour, gave special treatment to other officers in order to keep the affair secret, and attempted to engage other women in sexual relationships. Moreover, she reported that the former acting police chief had inappropriate relationships with both co-workers and police informants, that he made sexist comments to her about "baking cookies," and that he had a former employee fired on "trumped up charges" after reporting sexual harassment. The plaintiff also reported that a captain had engaged in workplace affairs. Consequently, the court, citing EEOC guidance as to favoritism constituting a hostile sexual environment, ruled that there was sufficient evidence to put the case before a jury to determine if sexual harassment occurred[34].

---

[33] EEOC, *Policy Guidance*, 1990, p. 5.
[34] *Nichol v. City of Springfield*, 2017, p. 54

To compare, in the federal district court case of *Garvin v. Southwestern Corr., LLC* (2019), the federal district court first held that widespread sexual favoritism could form the basis for a sexual harassment Title VII lawsuit, but after looking at the "totality of the circumstances" there were insufficient facts demonstrated to indicate that the sexual favoritism was so pervasive in the workplace so as to create an abusive and hostile working environment. In the case, the plaintiff, a female, prison transport officer, alleged that the warden of the prison, a male, and her supervisor, treated preferentially a co-worker with whom there was a "common belief" among the employees that he was having a sexual relationship with. The plaintiff alleged that the warden's paramour was given a preferential job title and a higher hourly rate for transporting prisoners, even though his paramour was purportedly significantly less qualified than the plaintiff. Moreover, the plaintiff alleged that the paramour was neither demoted nor received a reduction in pay when she refused to carry a weapon, which was a job requirement, Furthermore, the plaintiff alleged that the warden teased her about her appearance, focusing in on "characteristically male traits," and he did this teasing in front of other employees as well as inmates. Also, the plaintiff contended that the paramour allegedly made comments about her (i.e., the paramour's) breasts and her relationship with the warden in front of the plaintiff[35]. The court noted that the aforementioned conduct and comments were "humiliating and boorish" as well as "inappropriate for the workplace," but, "even if true," these allegations were inadequate to establish the requisite severe and pervasive harassment for a hostile environment case. The court further explained that the plaintiff named only one person, the

---

[35] *Garvin v. Southwestern Corr., LLC*, 2019.

co-worker, who was treated favorably because of her alleged sexual relationship with the warden, her supervisor, and "this does not support the inference of widespread sexual favoritism. Instead this appears to be an isolated instance of favoritism, which…courts have held to be insufficient to show a hostile work environment"[36].

One final example is the federal district court case of *Kelly v. Howard I. Shapiro & Assocs. Consulting Eng'rs, P.C.*, (2012), where the plaintiff, a female and company comptroller and office manager, was the supervisor of a mid-level female employee who engaged in a relationship with the company vice-president. The plaintiff claimed that because of the relationship the paramour was allowed to consistently violate company policy, that when the plaintiff tried to enforce those policies, the plaintiff was reprimanded, and she was undermined in her ability to do her job. The plaintiff claimed she was forced to leave the company; whereupon she sued, asserting hostile work environment and sex discrimination claims in violation of Title VII. The court, however, denied these claims, explaining that the plaintiff was not treated unequally because of her gender but due to the lack of a romantic relationship, and consequently there was no prohibited sex discrimination. Moreover, the conduct complained of consisted of isolated acts of preferential treatment due to a romantic relationship, which the court described as "paramour preference"; and the court underscored that the law is "well-settled" that such conduct is not actionable under Title VII. Finally, the court explained that the fact that the challenged conduct involved office romance and sexuality

---

[36] *Garvin v. Southwestern Corr., LLC*, 2019, p. 16.

did not, absent evidence of severe and pervasive sexual conduct, constitute a hostile work environment[37].

Therefore, to concisely conclude, one legal, though not necessarily moral, line is clearly between sexual conduct that is coerced as opposed to consensual. Another line is the one between isolated as opposed to widespread sexual favoritism. The cases indicate that for there to be a finding of a hostile sexual environment the romantic relationships and preferential conduct must be severe or egregious and pervasive or generalized, particularly conduct between a manager or supervisor and a subordinate employee. Pearce and Lipin (2015) conclude that "because of the difficulties inherent in providing these types of evidence, plaintiffs usually fail to prove the existence of a hostile work environment" (p. 334). Accordingly, an employer is allowed on an "isolated" basis to show favoritism and to bestow special benefits or grant preferential treatment to an employee based on a consensual love interest or an office romance relationship. Nevertheless, sexual favoritism, specifically, as well as sexual harassment and discrimination generally, are naturally caused by and complicated - legally, morally, and practically - by romance in the workplace.

Accordingly, the next legal section to this book will discuss some of the legal aspects of office romance with ethical analysis and practical suggestions provided in later sections.

---

[37] *Kelly v. Howard I. Shapiro & Assocs. Consulting Eng'rs, P.C.*, 2012, pp. 19-20.

3

Office Romance and Sexual Favoritism

This section to this book discusses the legal aspects of office romance which will be followed with ethical analysis and practical suggestions. We start by differentiating a complaint from a problem. A problem could be the more pervasive issue that is repeatedly causing certain inappropriate behaviors, actions, and sexual harassment challenges in the workplace.

Complaint vs· Problem

The saying "Where there is smoke, there is fire" has much truth to it. When someone complains of smoke in the room or in the building, managers must first focus on everyone's safety and then quickly find the actual fire so they can put it out, and thereby end all the smoke. Experts[38] have emphasized that any complaint about sexual harassment should not be confused with the harassment problem, because "When hostile work environment sexual harassment occurs, it is symptomatic of a

---

[38] Dobrich, Dranoff, and Maatman, 2002, p. 51.

more pervasive problem with employee respect in the company" or department's culture.

If there are legitimate complaints about workplace romance and favoritism in a department or specific organizational culture, then the workplace is probably contaminated with such thoughts, actions, and behaviors that could lead to sexual favoritism or harassment, inequity, and/or a hostile work environment. As such, a complaint should be welcomed with "open arms" by managers and human resource professionals since it could signal a problematic organizational culture where sexual favoritism or other discriminatory practices could be pervasive. Preventing sexual favoritism or sexual harassment requires discovering the root cause of the problem, fixing it through training or practical policies, and mitigating against any inappropriate actions quickly, consistently, and equitably for the safety of everyone in the organization.

When a complaint is launched, the manager's job is to reassure everyone that sexual favoritism or sexual harassment is not tolerated in the department, and that management will do everything possible to create a safe work environment for all. The manager must remain neutral and treat all employees (the accused as well as the accuser) with respect, dignity, and empathy. The manager's job is to be impartial and make sure all employees have relevant interpersonal skills in working with each other without any harassment or exclusionary tactics toward others based on their gender. The job of the human resource department is to document the complaint of sexual favoritism or harassment, thoroughly investigate it, and provide corrective actions as required by the policy of the company and existing laws. The starting point of investigating any complaint and finding the root cause can be to consider the legal aspects of sexual favoritism.

Legal Aspects

For an employer, legal as well as practical problems certainly are exacerbated by office romance and any resulting sexual favoritism. Yet, realistically, for an employer to try to "stamp out office romance is like standing in front of a speeding train," particularly because the workplace consistently comes up in surveys as the "number one" place to meet a mate[39]. The reasons are simple, that is, people at work spend a great deal of time together, they have similar interests, and they get to know each other very well; and the more familiar they are with each other the greater the likelihood of the co-workers being attracted to one another and thus to become romantically involved[40]. To illustrate, a 2017 Gallup poll revealed that 70% of the workers surveyed said they had a "meaningful relationship" at work[41]. Similarly, Byun (2014) reports on a survey that indicates that one-third of romantic relationships may begin in the workplace (p. 259, note 1). These workplace relationships may be "deeply meaningful connections, such as in the case of having a "work spouse," which describes a close relationship which is "equality-reinforcing and of mutual benefit"[42]. Positive benefits certainly can ensue from such a relationship, such as reducing stress and turnover, improving engagement and performance, and promoting productivity. However, these close friendship bonds can quickly turn into

---

[39] Shellenbarger, 2010, p. D1.
[40] Gallo, 2019.
[41] Kreis, 2020, p. 183.
[42] Kreis, 2020, p. 183.

workplace sexual and romantic relationships, and for employees of varying sexual orientations too, and these relationships can engender sexual favoritism in the workplace, which can result in sexual harassment and sexual discrimination. Consequently, as Kreis (2020, p. 184) emphasizes: "The positive gains notwithstanding, mixing pleasure with business can be a dangerous situation. Close friendships in professional settings can also cause conflict" as well as engender "hurt feelings, anger, and envy," thereby resulting in adverse employment conduct, including illegal conduct.

Office romance can certainly pose other major problems for employers, particularly if office romance causes sexual favoritism in the workplace. Office romances can have a negative "spillover effect" on co-workers. An example provided by Shellenbarger (2010, p. D1) is the experience of two co-workers who commenced dating. Initially they were considered to be equals on the job, with each other and their co-workers; but when the two started to go out to lunch regularly, their co-workers felt "excluded," which created "a lot of negativity." Office romance can also engender conflicts-of-interest as other employees may claim sexual favoritism if they feel they were not treated fairly because of a manager's preference to his or her romantic partner. Another problem with office romance is the potential for "messy breakups," perhaps resulting in allegations of sexual harassment and discrimination and thus consequently lawsuits. A study conducted by the Society for Human Resource Professionals, indicated that 67% of the employees surveyed cited as a significant problem the possibility of retaliation by "spurned or disappointed[43] lovers."

---

[43] Shellenbarger, 2010, pp. D1, D2.

Another way to avoid legal problems is for the employer to require that anyone who decides to embark on a dating relationship with another employee must disclose that relationship to human resources and then also require that the dating co-workers sign a contract that their romantic relationship is a consensual one. These contracts are at times called "love contracts," which will be more fully discussed in the "Recommendations" section. Suffice-it-to-say for now, if the romantic relationship ends poorly, that is, "crashes and burns," the contract should serve as a device to protect[44] the employer from sexual harassment and discrimination lawsuits. Yet, the employer also must be aware that such a policy may cause other legal problems for the employer because if the information regarding the dating relationship, which certainly can be construed as private and personal, is improperly accessed and/or disclosed publicly, the employer could face a lawsuit for the intentional tort of invasion of privacy, particularly if the disclosure adversely affects the employees' ability to obtain another job.

Nevertheless, regardless of employer policies, workplace dating and office romance are, as emphasized, "unavoidable" since employees, who are often like-minded and have similar interests, and spend so much time together, naturally will develop close bonds. Thus, human nature being what it is, the employer must be cognizant of the fact that realistically it would be impossible to totally prevent employees from engaging in office romances. Clearly, what is necessary is for the employer to be proactive and thus to promulgate clear, concise, understandable, and fair office romance policies that set forth appropriate romantic relationship standards and proper

---

[44] Cavico, Mujtaba, and Samuels, 2012.

conduct. We will suggest and discuss such policies in the "Recommendations" section of this book.

Implications

We can summarize that, legally, the general rule is that sexual favoritism is not actionable as illegal sexual discrimination and/or harassment. However, as emphasized, there are two important exceptions, to wit: sexual favoritism may rise to the level of a Title VII violation when the practice adversely affects employment opportunities for third parties and the sexual favoritism is deemed to be coercive *"quid pro quo"* sexual harassment and/or hostile work environment harassment. Significantly, in a hostile environment case the pervasive sexual conduct that creates the hostile work environment can do so for those employees who find it offensive or abusive even if the perpetrator only targets employees who welcome the sexual conduct and even if there is no sexual conduct directed against the employee bringing the claim. However, absent a hostile environment, and if a manager or supervisor does not force an applicant or employee to submit to sexual advances in order to obtain a job or gain a promotion, then the situation is "merely" one of sexual favoritism or "paramour preference" and thus not, according to the courts and EEOC, legally impermissible sexual harassment. Allowing office romance, however, means more interpersonal relations between co-workers in the workplace, and thus likely more romantic relationships and as a result perhaps more sexual favoritism, which can cause legal as well as practical problems for the employer. Yet, even if dating in the workplace among employees is permitted and any resulting sexual favoritism occurs, it is generally legal. Nonetheless the ethical questions remain as to the morality of office romance and sexual favoritism, which perforce brings one into the realm of philosophical ethics.

Ethical Analysis

An analysis of the current state of the law regarding sexual favoritism in the workplace in the context of office romance indicates that there are shortcomings in the ability of the legal system to address sexual favoritism and regulate office romance in the workplace. Accordingly, the question arises as to what is the moral course of conduct for an employer to take? Such an inquiry perforce takes one into the realm of ethics, a branch of philosophy.

As a start for reflection, the model of communication ethics in Figure 3 by Mainiero and Jones (2013, p. 372) for 'ethical' decision-making addresses potential implications of sexual contacts between coworkers. Given the prevalence or widespread existence of workplace romance, and the fears of managers that some workplace romances will turn into harassment, Mainiero and Jones emphasize that it is important to provide an ethical model to represent the standards, that is, what is appropriate, and what is inappropriate workplace behavior when employees are involved in romantic relationships. Mainiero and Jones's model is intended to guide behavior that fall in the gray area, which they define as "romantic communications that escape the direct legal standard of harassment (which would require organizational action) but nonetheless are perceived as bothersome or intrusive to an employee in or outside the office" (2013a, p. 372). They have constructed the Communication Ethics Model of Workplace Romance to guide employees to consider the communication ethics of their workplace romance actions.

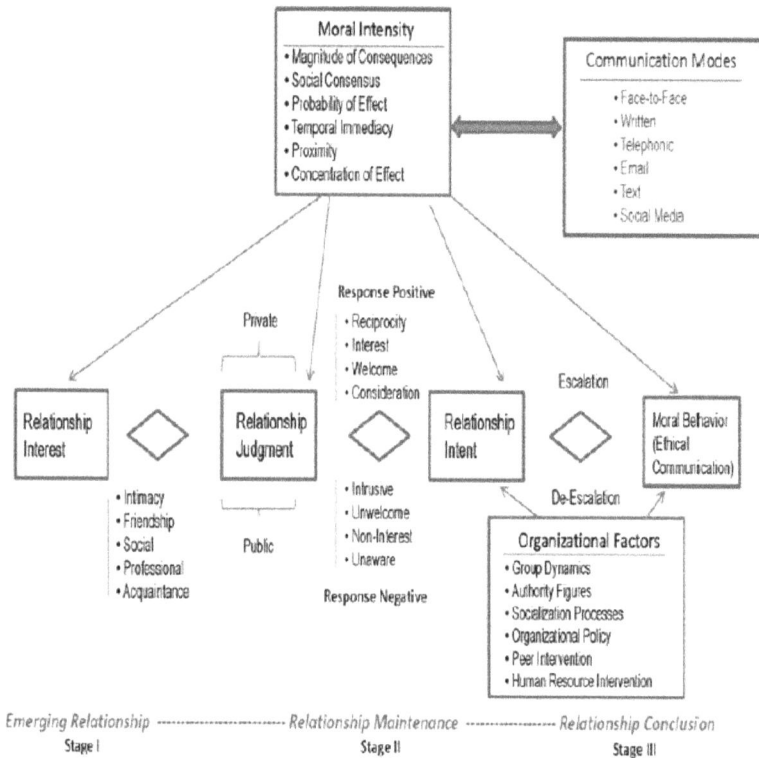

Figure 3 – Communication Ethics of Workplace Romance
(Lisa A. Mainiero and Kevin J. Jones, 2013a, p. 372)

In this chapter, to look at the practical side of ethics related to workplace romance, we will discuss and then apply the four major, secular, reasoned-based ethical theories in Western Civilization – Ethical Egoism, Ethical Relativism, Utilitarianism, and Kantian ethics. – in order to make some moral determinations regarding office romance and any attendant sexual favoritism. The first ethical theory to be discussed is Ethical Egoism.

Ethical Egoism

Ethical Egoism is an ethical theory first propounded by the ancient Greeks, being originally attributed to the philosophic school of the Sophists in 5th century B.C., who were egoists and relativists in their thinking. The modern, relatively speaking, proponent of this ethical theory is the 18th century English economist Adam Smith. The basic tenet of ethical egoism maintains that it is moral to advance one's self-interest; and thus in a business context it is moral to make money. That is, an action that advances one's self-interest is a moral one; and, conversely, an action that is detrimental to one's self-interest is an immoral one. As *per* Adam Smith's rationale, if everyone seeks to advance their self-interest not only will they benefit, but society and the general welfare will benefit also as there will be more efficient and effective production and distribution of goods and services. Yet there are some constraints on the doctrine. First, is to take a long-term perspective as to maximizing one's self-interest, and thus be willing to undergo some short-term sacrifice, expense, and effort in order to maximize one's own long-term greater good. Second, generally, it is preferable to treat people well, to make them part of one's team, in essence, to co-op them. And why should one be so "nice"? Because it is in one's long-term self-interest to have friends and allies as opposed to enemies. So, Adam Smith asserted that one should be selfish in the egoistic sense, but do so in a smart, prudent, and rational manner. That is, be an enlightened ethical egoist, but advance oneself, learn useful knowledge and skills, and become wealthy and powerful. Therefore, Ethical Egoism, defines morality as advancing one's self-interest; in essence, it is moral to make money (but remember to take a long-term perspective as to maximizing your self-interest, and thus also be willing to undergo some short-term expense and effort, as well as to treat people well).

Office romances certainly can present major problems and challenges for the affected employees and particularly for the ethically egoistic employer, especially when office romance results in sexual favoritism and sexual harassment. Kreis (2020) explains: "When office romances sour or illicit workplace relationships are discovered, those dynamics are problematic for corporate decision-makers, especially when they involve a supervisor and a subordinate employee. Under these circumstances, adverse employment consequences may fall on subordinate employees because supervisors are spurned lovers, resentful, or desperate to save another preexisting relationship or marriage" (p. 188). Moreover, adverse consequences can also fall on the employer in the form of sexual harassment lawsuits if sexual relationships are coerced and/or the granting of sexual favors is widely expected to obtain promotions and other job benefits. Green (2019) underscores that "corporations need to recognize that sexual harassers do incredible harm to their companies. Even a top-performing executive who harasses subordinates is not worth the harm to the employer's bottom line" (p. 147). Thus, an important consideration for management to ponder is whether the consent in a relationship between a manager or supervisor and subordinate employee is in fact genuine, due to the power imbalance in the relationship. For the ethically egoistic employer, therefore, the responsibility – morally as well as legally and practically – falls to ensure a fair, just, and functional workplace. Particular attention must be paid to potential dating relationships between managers and supervisors and subordinate employees. We propose certain "egoistic" suggestions, first, generally, to combat sexual harassment and discrimination as well as sexual favoritism and second, specifically, to achieve fair and efficacious office romance policies. Ethical Egoism is obviously a narrowly based egoistic and "selfish" ethical doctrine; whereas the next ethical theory to be considered – Ethical Relativism – is a much broader societal-based ethical doctrine.

Ethical Relativism

"When in Rome, do as the Romans do." Surely you have heard of this famous statement, though perhaps not always reflecting on fully understanding its ethical implications. As such, that old saying is a good introduction to the ethical theory of Ethical Relativism, which harkens back before the Romans to a later group of the Sophists in ancient Greece. The key aspect of this ethical theory is that morality is determined by societal beliefs, mores, and precepts. That is, what a society believes is moral for that society is in fact moral for that society. Consequently, one does not need to be a philosopher to determine morality; rather, one needs "sharp" eyes-and-ears to discern what the moral standards are "on the ground" in a particular society. One "merely" must get educated as to the prevailing moral norms in the relevant society. Then one just must conform to and adopt those norms and one will be acting morally in that society. Naturally, one does not want to get educated the "hard way" by gratuitously and foolishly contravening some local societal moral norm; so, the astute businessperson will always check with the appropriate local people "on the ground" in the pertinent society. Of course, two societies can disagree about moral norms. As a result, a weakness of this ethical theory is that there is no arbitrating mechanism to say which society's moral beliefs are objectively and absolutely true and correct. Yet they are true and correct for that society, so one should merely conform and adopt and be moral there, and one should not be a "cultural imperialist" and consequently try to impose one's own society's moral views on another. Another weakness of Ethical Relativism is trying to determine exactly what the critical component of "society" is. Now, such a determination may be a bit easier in a very homogenous society but certainly not a heterogeneous one. Consequently, in the business context herein, what is the relevant society – global business, U.S. business – as a whole or regionally, a particular industry, a particular company, a particular facility, division, department, or even a team of a company? As such, some companies in some locales may have in their discrete definitions of "society" a more "free-wheeling," "free-love" atmosphere regarding office romance among employees whereas other firms may be more strict, rigid, and prohibitive in their dating policies.

Generally, in the authors' opinions, before the advent of the #MeToo movement office romance (so long as consensual, of course) had become less taboo; thus, the practice had been treated as more acceptable at certain companies, but certainly not all companies. Office romance has been "coming out of the closet," and the workplace thus had become a "place for courtship." In 2010, before the advent of the #MeToo movement, it was reported on a survey[45] in which 67% of employees stated they had no need to hide their office relationships, which figure was up from 54% five years earlier. Baby-Boomers kept their office romances secret, in part because of fears of career damage, reprisal, and sanctions, particularly since many employers had policies strictly forbidding office romances, at least between people in the different management ranks or hierarchy. Yet societal mores had been changing regarding office dating. There was more openness about dating, romance, and sex as well as more equality between the sexes. Nonetheless, it was then and most certainly now, still considered to be inappropriate for married employees to date other co-workers, as well as for dating co-workers to engage in displays of affection in the workplace. Even the most liberal employer would expect, and demand, that employees who are dating behave in a professional manner; and most employers also would say that it still would be considered inappropriate for a boss and a subordinate employee to date[46].

In order to get a sense for more recent, post-#MeToo, societal mores, Weiss (2019) noted the findings of several studies: "Public opinion seems solidly supportive of office romance: one survey found that only 4% believe that work relationships are wrong under all circumstances. Indeed, between a third and a half of respondents reported having had sexual or romantic involvement at work. Yet surveys also suggest that attraction and relationships between supervisor and subordinate can be problematic even when genuinely motivated by affection. These relationships account for just under 10% of

---

[45] Shellenbarger, 2010, p. D2
[46] Shellenbarger, 2010.

office relationships and are disproportionately dangerous" (pp. 321-22). Moreover, "public opinion is less approving of relationships between co-workers and subordinates, though only a minority (43%) feel that relationships between supervisors and subordinates are never appropriate" (Weiss, 2019, p. 322). Leong (2019) points to a survey which indicates that 64% of respondents believed that a supervisor should not be having sex with a subordinate employee (p. 954). Nevertheless, Weiss (2019) points to a survey which indicated that 22% of employees have dated someone who was their supervisor at the time (p. 322). Similarly, Leong (2019) reports on surveys which indicated that 35.6% of respondents said that they have had sex with a subordinate and 15% saying that they had dated a supervisor (pp. 951-52). Yet, Weiss (2019) also reports on a Harris poll which found that 31% of employees surveyed who started dating at work eventually married (p. 322, note 111). Accordingly, if there is an overly restrictive policy on office romance and such a prohibitive policy becomes widespread, then many people will find it difficult to embark on long-term relationships and to find marriage partners[47]. Therefore, based on the admittedly anecdotal evidence and the authors' own knowledge and experience it seems, generally, that pursuant to Ethical Relativism the prevailing societal moral norms would be to allow limited dating and office romance so long as it is conducted in a professional manner, rather than fully prohibiting dating between a manager or supervisor and a subordinate employee. Yet, what type of office romance policies achieve the "greater good," so as to be moral under the next ethical theory – Utilitarianism.

---

[47] Leong, 2019,

Utilitarianism

Utilitarianism is an ethical theory created by the 18th Century English philosophers and social reformers - Jeremy Bentham and John Stuart Mill. The theory is a consequentialist ethical theory; that is, morality is determined by focusing in on all the stakeholders (also called "constituent groups) affected by the action. There is a predictive element to this ethical theory; that one must predict consequences as they affect each discrete stakeholder group, including society as a whole. Ethical Egoism is of course a consequentialist ethical theory too, but plainly with Utilitarianism the scope of analysis is much, much broader than merely oneself. Predicting the consequences of an action is obviously a challenging task, but the Utilitarians say, first, to use one's "common storehouse of knowledge" and to use "history as a guide." Second, one needs to look for probabilities of occurrences as well as the reasonably foreseeable consequences of putting an action into effect. Finally, one must attempt to measure and weigh consequences, first, for each stakeholder group and then among all the stakeholders. Accordingly, if there are predominantly good consequences the action is a moral action; and conversely, if there are mostly negative consequences the action is an immoral one. The goal of the Utilitarians was to seek to promote happiness, satisfaction, and pleasure; but note that since the "ends justify the means" there can be some painful consequences produced, but overall if there is more good an action can be deemed moral. However, one problem with this theory is that the "ends can justify means"; that is, if there is more good than bad the action is moral even though there are some consequences that cause pain, suffering, and unhappiness consistently to a specific stakeholder group. Depending on the company and its office romance polices and the existence of sexual favoritism, a plethora of consequences – good and bad – can emanate from those policies. As such, the authors will point out some of the reasonably foreseeable consequences, attempt to measure and weigh them, and thus decide where the "greater good" lies.

Initially, office romance can result in some *positive* consequences in the workplace, to wit: workplace romance can enhance attitude toward work, happiness, motivation, and "engagement," that is, the desire and excitement to come to work, to care about one's company, and to work diligently[48]. A positive effect of office romance is that it can lead to increased productivity for both participants. Furthermore, romantically involved co-workers typically spend more time at work, take fewer days off, and are less likely to be absent and to quit. There also may be an increase in coordination, group-work, and teamwork, as well as creativity and dynamism. The possibility of finding a romantic partner at work should naturally make the work environment an enjoyable, even exciting, one. The romantically involved co-workers may be more motivated to come to work, and to work. Interaction and communication at work certainly should be increased. Leong (2019) submits that workplace romance creates a more exciting workplace as well as more energized work and team groups, enhances communication and cooperation, stimulates creativity, and thus produces a "happier work environment" (p. 983). Therefore, some companies, such as National Public Radio, Princeton Review, Pixar, and Southwest Airlines, encourage office romance among employees[49].

---

[48] Morgan, 2010.
[49] Morgan, 2010.

However, office romance can also result in *negative* consequences for employers, co-workers, and the romantically involved employees. Initially it is important to note that a great deal of these positive consequences potentially emanating from office romance assume that the romantic co-workers, as well as their colleagues for that matter, will be open, mature, and professional about the relationship. Yet, dating among co-workers may be disruptive to the work environment, both during the dating period but particularly during any breakup. Office romance can adversely affect the productivity of the workers romantically involved as well as the morale and productivity of their co-workers. If the dating co-workers are having a difficult time with their romantic relationship, this "lover's quarrel" may intrude on the workplace, consequently making their co-workers feel uncomfortable and less productive[50]. Unwanted sexual advances and conduct can adversely affect the victim's ability to do his or her job. Moreover, if such conduct is pervasive other employees might be intimidated by such a highly sexualized work atmosphere, which perforce could degenerate into a hostile, and thus illegal, work environment. Sexual favoritism can have adverse effects on third-party employees in the workplace. As such, Byun (2014) asserts the following: "Third-party employees – those employees who do not enjoy a particular benefit because they are not inclined to become romantically involved with a superior – may feel threatened and uncomfortable as a result of the flirtatious, sexual, or romantic conduct of the supervisor and participating employee. Sexual favoritism may lead to lower office morale, as employees may become jealous and feel angry about officemates who use their sexuality to gain benefits" (pp.

---

[50] Cavico, Mujtaba, and Samuels, 2012.

268-269). Byun (2014) also warns that "an angry third party may act hostile toward the employee who receives sexual favoritism" (p. 269). These adverse effects on third parties can be especially severe when the relationship is a superior-subordinate one. Leong (2019) thus contends that "a supervisor-subordinate relationship that is going badly can be more uncomfortable for third parties because of the power disparity involved" (p. 962).

Sexual favoritism and "paramour preference" undermine the merit principle in the workplace. As such, Leong (2019) asserts that "it is unsurprising that sexual favoritism produces a negative psychological effect on third parties in the institution," particularly by vitiating the "meritocracy" principle in the workplace (p. 961). "Favoritism" thus can emerge as a contentious issue as employees tend to believe that favoritism exists when there is a romantic relationship between employees, particularly a manager or a supervisor and a subordinate employee. Favoritism, or even the perception thereof, can engender dislike, disapproval, even hostility among co-workers, especially regarding the receipt of promotions or other benefits or preferential treatment. Byun (2014) emphasizes that "the primary concern is that employees are being assessed according to their sexual conduct rather than their work capabilities" (p. 268). Certain surveys underscore the negative consequences for employees. For example, Morgan (2010), indicated that in a 2010 survey, 75% of U.S. workers surveyed by job search website Monster.com believed a workplace relationship could bring a conflict; and 62% said they felt office romances were a distraction from job performance.

Office gossip very likely will be increased and intensified by office romance[51]. A deleterious work environment of disharmony, negativity, and cynicism could be spawned by an office romance. The legal and practical adverse consequences to office romance could have a "chilling effect" on interpersonal relations in the workplace. Weiss (2019) explains the potential negative repercussions:

> When sexual advances are rejected or relationships are ended, the rejected party may experience pain, shame, anger, resentment, or feelings of inadequacy. A rejected supervisor may thus have difficulty treating a subordinate fairly. Fearing this, a subordinate who wishes to reject or end sexual contact may suffer great anxiety and may feel intimidated into sex even when there is not direct threat of harm. Rejected parties may feel this full range of emotions regardless of their original intent: rejection is not fun whether advances were motived by love, lust, or animus (p. 331).

Many employees, moreover, might believe that a workplace relationship could bring a conflict-of-interest situation; and others could feel that office romances are a distraction from and impediment to job performance. Customers of the employer could be affected in a negative manner if the romantically involved co-workers are paying too much attention to each other as opposed to serving the needs of the employer's customers. Poor customer service will of course "translate" into fewer customers and consequently less revenue for the employer.

---

[51] Leong, 2019.

Sexual favoritism especially if widespread can create a "sexualized" workplace. Consequently, Leong (2019) warns as follows:

> A sexualized institutional environment desensitizes members of the institution to various sexual abuses. Workers who see a supervisor casually engage in sexual relationships with multiple partners may view it as a license to cross other boundaries. They may assume that the institution has a more relaxed view when it comes to sexual harassment; they may feel more entitled to tell inappropriate stories; to feel more empowered to ask for dates aggressively and repeatedly. These harms do not fall on women only, but they disproportionately affect women (p. 969).

The aforementioned negative consequences certainly can be exacerbated when managers or supervisors date subordinate employees. Byun (2014) counsels that "sexual favoritism can also be damaging to the party consenting to – or initiating – the flirtatious or sexual conduct with his or her supervisor. While the subordinate employee's relationship with the supervisor may be consensual, the employee also may feel intimidated, fearing repercussions if they lose interest or if the relationship ends" (p. 269). Managers and supervisors who engage in widespread sexual favoritism will not only cause legal problems but also send a "loud and clear" and value-destroying message in the workplace that the way for women to get a position, promotion, or job benefit is to engage in sexual conduct; that is, to submit to sexual solicitations is a prerequisite to any type of objective or fair treatment. One cannot think of a more morale-destroying set of circumstances. Sexual harassment lawsuits are also more prevalent when supervisor-subordinate relationships end. Weiss (2019) explains as follows:

> The perils of romance in the supervisory setting are attested by the significant number of sexual harassment cases involving a defendant whose feelings about the plaintiff seem, on any reasonable interpretation, to have been sincere and romantic interest. In some cases, the plaintiff had originally engaged in a consensual affair. In others the defendant's interest in the plaintiff was never reciprocated. In either situation, the plaintiff eventually rejected the defendant. At that point, the defendant began to engage in workplace behavior that was harmful to the plaintiff. Sometimes the behavior in these cases is merely wounded – such as avoidance of direct contact that led to less favorable work assignments. In other cases, the behavior was more antagonistic but would not in itself have risen to the threshold need for a hostile environment claim (p. 322).

However, another negative consequence, particularly for female employees, can arise if a company has a too stringent policy regarding office romance is that the policy, in order to reduce the risk of sexual favoritism and sexual harassment liability, may inhibit the contacts between male and female employees. One, perhaps unintended, result that would be harmful to women because they may be deprived of valuable exposure to higher level male employees, for example, travelling and dining with men, as well as concomitantly decreased mentoring and networking opportunities. Consequently, Kreis (2020) warns: "For women in the workforce such avoidance tactics like this create defensive glass ceilings; these practices isolate women and stunt their growth trajectories while perpetuating stereotypes" (p. 152). Furthermore, severe restrictions on contact could exacerbate the fears of male employees that they will be tempted to overstep some boundary – legal, moral, or marital with their female colleagues. Men, moreover, may fear that simply the appearance of a romantic or sexual liaison or relationship and the perceived attendant jealousy, harm to reputation, and concerns with sexual favoritism and conflicts-of-interest[52]. Since it is nearly impossible for an employer to stop the employees from engaging in romantic relationships, a policy that is too strict a prohibition may actually cause more harm than good consequences. As a result of strict policies, the employees may feel compelled to hide their dating relationship, and this secrecy could cause even greater problems when management and/or co-workers discover the relationship, and perhaps the "preferences" that accompanied the relationship.

Pursuant to the Utilitarian analysis, therefore, the seminal question is where is the "greater good"? Adopting a free and open office romance policy appears to cause predominant negative consequences for the employer, its employees, and other stakeholders, and thus should be eschewed as immoral pursuant to Utilitarian ethics. However, a policy that allows dating but with the important exception of a prohibition of dating between managers or supervisors and subordinate employees seems to strike the right balance and

---

[52] Kreis, 2020.

achieves more good consequences than bad, and thus would be the moral course of action under Utilitarianism. Of course, there will be some negative consequences for the affected romantic parties, and the Utilitarians would say to try to mitigate these bad consequences. So, perhaps, a prohibition but with the option of one of paramours transferring within the company to a different hierarchical management structure in another facility, division, department, or team would go a long way in lessening the harm of the prohibition. Yet, regardless of whether an action or policy achieves any "greater good" there is nonetheless one more (at least pursuant to ethics in Western Civilization) ethical test to apply to determine the morality of the action or policy – Kantian ethics.

Kantian Ethics

Kantian ethics is the philosophical moral theory propounded by the German philosopher and professor, Immanuel Kant. Kantian ethics is premised on reason, duty, and autonomy. Kant reasoned that morality is not based on the consequences of an action (thus directly contradicting Utilitarianism), but rather on examining the action itself and whether the action passes a formal test, which Kant called the Categorical Imperative. Furthermore, Kant asserts that the Categorical Imperative is the only, true, and supreme ethical test for determining morality. Therefore, regardless of how many "good" consequences an action produces, if the action fails the Categorical Imperative, it is an immoral action. As such, the "ends do NOT justify the means" in Kantian ethics; rather, the means themselves must be moral. Accordingly, in order to determine if an action is moral, the formal test of the Categorical Imperative must be applied to the action. It is important to note that the Categorical is not only reason-created and -based, but it is imposed on a person not by the law or the dictates of any government, but freely and willingly by a person who first, acting rationally and logically realizes that the Categorical Imperative is the only true measure of morality, and second, by a person who also has the free will, autonomy, and strength of character to do what the Categorical Imperative tells him or her what is the moral thing to do, and to not do what the Categorical Imperative tells him or her is the immoral thing to do.

Moreover, to be sure, very sure, that an action is moral, the Categorical Imperative has three parts or tests that must be applied, and all three must be passed for a moral conclusion; and thus, if the action fails one test it is immoral. The three parts to the *Categorical Imperative* are:

    1) the Universal Law test,
    2) the Kingdom of Ends test, and
    3) the Agent-Receiver test.

Pursuant to the *Universal Law test* an action is moral only if it can be made universally consistent as a moral "law" or precept. Consequently, if when made universally consistent the action cannot sustain itself and self-destructs, the action is immoral. Kant used lying and cheating as examples because they cannot be made universally consistent. That is, if everyone lied because "lying" was the "moral" norm, then no one would ever believe anyone else, and thus lying would lose its efficaciousness, and thereby self-destruct. Lying, therefore, is immoral, as is cheating based on the same logical type of analysis. Pursuant to the second test, which Kant called the *Kingdom of Ends test*, an action is only moral if it treats people as worthwhile human beings deserving and entitled to dignified and respectful treatment. Consequently, if an action treats a person as a thing, tool, instrument, or means to achieve some end, the action is undignified and disrespectful, and thus immoral even if it results in some type of greater good. Finally, pursuant to the third test of the Categorical Imperative, which Kant called the *Agent-Receiver test* (and which he conveniently borrowed and made secular from the Golden Rule of the Bible), Kant asks one to consider the contemplated action and then to ask if one did not know one would be the agent, that is, the giver of the action, or its receiver, would one be willing to have that action done; and if not the action is immoral. That is, "do unto to others as one would want done to oneself".

So, how do Kantian ethics apply when employment decisions are being made and benefits granted, not because of an employee's knowledge, skills, and capabilities, but because the employee is romantically involved with a manager, supervisor, or co-worker. Pursuant to Kant's supreme test of ethics, the Categorical Imperative, such sexual favoritism is patently unfair and demeaning and disrespectful treatment and conduct in the workplace and thus is immoral. First, pursuant to the "Universal Law" test of the Categorical Imperative, sexual favoritism or "paramour preference" cannot be made into a consistent universal moral norm of "law" since the action logically is not sustainable if applied universally; rather, it self-destructs; that is, no one would want to work for a company in which the governing "moral" norm is sex-supersedes-qualifications-merit; and thus there would be no workforce (or a very, very limited workforce), and thus no employees and no company. Sexual favoritism also fails the second test of the Categorical Imperative, the Kingdom of Ends test, as the employee who is being discriminated against and denied benefits because he or she refuses to have sex with a manager or supervisor is certainly not being treated with dignity and respect; and actually the paramour of the manager or supervisor can also be treated in a undignified and disrespectful manner as a sex object, and not as a worthwhile human being, especially if there is even a "hint" of compulsion to the relationship due to the disparity of the parties involved. Finally, the Agent-Receiver test of the Categorical Imperative is being violated since what rational person would enter into an employment situation not knowing whether he or she would be the romantically involved co-worker, the preferred paramour, or the third-party employee being denied benefits due to preferences being granted to the paramour.

Moreover, even if women (or men) are not directly subject to sexual conduct, if requests for sexual favors are widespread in the workplace a demeaning message is sent to all employees that management regards women (or men) as merely means or instruments to fulfill manager's or supervisor's sexual wants and needs; and consequently that the required way for women (or men) to get ahead in the workplace is to engage in sexual conduct – voluntarily or involuntarily – with management. Such a sexual environment at work is demeaning and disrespectful to the employees and treats them as mere "things" of a sexual nature and not as worthwhile human beings deserving of dignity and respect. Widespread sexual harassment, therefore, is demeaning to all people in the workplace – women as well as men – and is therefore immoral. Moreover, widespread sexual favoritism treats women as sexual objects and such conduct also sends a message that the way for women to advance in the workplace and to be treated fairly is that they must engage in sex[53]. Yet Kreis (2020) notes: "While fundamentally unjust, a romantic relationship's negative externalities, like the fallout from broken romances, are not actionable sex-based discrimination" under the legal law (p. 189).

There is, however, a philosophical duality in Kantian ethics. The two cardinal principles in the Categorical Imperative are first, respect and dignity for and by human beings, and second, the autonomy and free will of rational human beings. The latter principle can also be triggered in an office romance situation. That is, a complete ban of dating relationships in the workplace, even beyond managers and supervisors and subordinate employees, "would intrude too much on the freedom of mature adults, who not infrequently choose to enter such relationships"[54]; and thus, such a ban would violate their autonomy and free will as rational human beings and consequently would violate Kantian ethics. Accordingly, it would be a moral course of conduct under Kantian ethics to allow the employees to date, but to clearly inform and remind them that they are adults in a professional setting and thus they must eschew any favoritism and conflicts-of-interest. As such, they should carefully consider the consequences of dating on themselves, their work colleagues, other third parties, and the company. As such, they should abjure public displays of affection and embarrassing conduct, and other inappropriate conduct that distracts other employees and hinders company operations, as well as avoid conflicts-of-interest and sexual favoritism (real or perceived); and the dating employees must always treat their co-workers, customers, and

---

[53] Leong, 2019.
[54] Weiss, 2019, p. 330.

clients, as well as each other with dignity and respect. Furthermore, if the dating relationship ends, the employees must still maintain that level of professionalism, dignity, and respect for each other, the company, and its stakeholders.

So, ethically, what is the moral course of conduct for the employer when it comes to sexual favoritism and office romance in the workplace? Such a determination takes one into the realm of "situational ethics," that is, morality being decided by not merely the different set of facts "on the ground", but also which ethical theory one is applying to the facts to make the moral determination, especially considering that the two major "modern" theories in Western Civilization – Utilitarianism and Kantian ethics, are diametrically opposed. Consequently, and not to be too "sophisticated" in the presentation and application of ethical theories (as *per* the Sophists of Ancient Greece and their emphasis on pure relativism), but at times the moral conclusion that one reasons to, and even legitimately and logically so, flows from the ethical theory one is applying to the moral question at issue. The authors trust that managers and employees have made some objective and well-reasoned moral conclusions based on the four ethical theories explicated and applied. Moreover, to be even more philosophical in determining the morality of the matters at hand – sexual favoritism and office romance – the authors would harken back to the Roman philosopher Ovid, who famously said "the middle road is the safest," as well as the Greek philosopher, Aristotle, and his ethical principle of the *Doctrine of the Mean*, wherein the smart as well as moral course of conduct is the one that is the "mean" between two extremes, for example, bravery (the right amount of courage) as the mean between cowardice (too little courage) and rashness (too much courage). Therefore, for sexual favoritism and office romance policies that are moral the authors submit that a company should avoid the extremes, that is, neither totally prohibit office romance nor have a wide-open dating policy, but rather find the mean, which logically should be prohibiting dating between managers and supervisors and their subordinate employees (yet with a transfer option), but allowing other employees to date under certain conditions, which we elaborate on in the "Recommendations," section to this book.

5

Recommendations

Initially, before discussing recommendations, it is important to note that one federal district court clearly advised employers as well as employees that the employment laws have neither vested the federal courts to sit as "super-personnel departments" nor to determine the "wisdom and fairness" of employer business decisions (*Morris v. Acadian Ambulance Servs.*, 2015). Accordingly, it is the principal function of a company's top management and Legal and Human Resources departments to ensure that business decisions, especially those affecting the employees, are wise, fair, moral, and, of course, legal. Employers, therefore, must be keenly aware of the legal, ethical, and practical implications of office romance and sexual favoritism and be ready and able to promulgate appropriate policies. Accordingly, we now submit the following practical, efficacious, and helpful recommendations.

Avoid Sexual Harassment

It is a fact that workplace romance and sexual favoritism have been on the rise in the United States of America. As such, it is important for organizations and managers to have relevant human resource (HR) policies regarding workplace romantic relationships in order to protect their employees from sexual harassment and discrimination, as well as to prevent the company from costly lawsuits. Clearly, any workplace romance has the potential for favoritism, especially when the relationship involves a manager and an employee. As such, it is a "best practice" for all organizations to ensure their workplace is free from sexual harassment. The following[55] are some general recommendations:

(a) Develop a policy that clearly states intolerance for sexual harassment.
(b) Provide training to senior and new employees to properly identify inappropriate workplace behaviors.
(c) Have a procedure in place that encouragingly allows for reporting sexual harassment in the workplace,
(d) Consistently discipline employees who commit sexual harassment.
(e) Take action to protect every victim of sexual assault, sexual harassment, or a hostile work environment.

Having such policies in place, communicating them often to all employees, and enforcing them consistently can generate, establish, and/or reinforce a healthy work environment for everyone and prevent potential lawsuits. Furthermore, such policies can also allow an organizational culture of open communication around sexual harassment in the workplace. Let us expand on these recommendations.

First and foremost, appropriate policies, programs, procedures, and training are necessary to combat sexual

---

[55] Noe et. al., 2021, p. 140.

discrimination and harassment and thus to ensure a fair, just, and functional workplace. However, very surprisingly, Call (2018) reports on a survey by XpertHr which indicated that 20% of the employers surveyed do not offer sexual harassment training. Yet, "prevention is the best tool for the elimination of sexual harassment" in the workplace[56]. In determining the adequacy of an employer's prevention methods, reference first should be made to the federal district court case of *Alatorre v. Mabus* (2015, p. 24), where the court emphasized that merely having an anti-discrimination and anti-harassment policy is insufficient; rather, the court set forth in general terms the basic components of an "effective" policy, to wit: a requirement that all employees, particularly, managers and supervisors, report instances of discrimination and harassment; allowing the employees to file informal as well as formal complaints; a reporting mechanism that permits an aggrieved employee to bypass a supervisor or manager; and providing sufficient training regarding the policy. Based on the preceding counsel from the court, the authors' own experiences and observations, as well as the suggestions from legal and management commentators[57], we submit the following recommendations:

The Code of Ethics or Code of Conduct for the workplace should include a clear and strong policy statement against sexual harassment and discrimination. Most importantly, the policy statement must include "a bold and direct statement of the intolerance and prohibition of any form of sexual harassment[58]" as well as discrimination. The code also should include a clear statement of as well as explanation of

---

[56] Pearce and Lipin, 2015, p. 347.
[57] see, for example, Farkas, *et. al.*, 2019; Flores, 2019; Houseman, 2019; Pearce and Lipin, 2015; Cavico, Mujtaba, and Samuels, 2012.
[58] Pearce and Lipin, 2015, p. 347.

prohibited conduct. The employer should have an effective policy distribution plan, including communication to and acknowledgement by the employees. There should be in the code a clear and effective complaint or reporting procedure that contains different avenues to complain. In addition, employers should take steps to promote the availability and use of these internal reporting systems. Moreover, there must be assurances that any complaint will be promptly and thoroughly investigated, and that the employer will protect the confidentiality of complaining employees to the extent possible. Finally, there must be very strong assurances that complaining employees will be protected from harassment or retaliation as well as that any such retribution will be severely punished.

In conjunction with the code and reporting mechanisms, establishing systemic investigative procedures which are objective, just, and fair is required. The employer must ensure that the investigative process affords all the parties involved a prompt, thorough, and fair investigation as well as a timely resolution of the complaint. If violations have occurred, corrective actions that are prompt and effective are essential. There should be a tiered or graduated system of violations with specified sanctions and penalties for violations. Assurances in the code must be given that the employer will take immediate and appropriate action in the form of proportionate discipline if there is a determination that harassment or discrimination has occurred. Finally, continual auditing and monitoring of personnel to ensure compliance as well as record-keeping of all complaints of harassment and discrimination is strongly recommended.

Specifically, regarding training, it first should be noted that many states[59] "encourage" employers to provide such training, as does the EEOC, but three states – California, Connecticut, and Maine – require businesses to implement comprehensive training programs that are designed to raise awareness of sexual harassment in the workplace and to prevent such misconduct. Regardless of any mandatory or "encouraged" training, the ethically egoistic employer should promulgate anti-discrimination and anti-harassment policies, conduct appropriate training, and establish secure reporting mechanisms. Such an effort will show that the employer is acting as a reasonably prudent employer legally as well as a moral employer ethically. Accordingly, education and training should be mandatory for all employees, especially officers, managers, and supervisors, as well as investigators. They all should be educated and trained as to the existence and provision of the company's Code of Ethics or Conduct, and how it applies to discrimination and harassment in the workplace. Education and training should also encompass the fundamentals of anti-discrimination and anti-harassment law. Investigators particularly should be educated as to the law of defamation and invasion of privacy law, and especially the legal risks pursuant to those laws during an investigation. Education and training can be conducted online, personally, in workshops, and/or group sessions. Managers and supervisors should be required[60] to formally acknowledge that they received the written anti-discrimination and anti-harassment policy as well as completed the requisite training, "and doing so, if they then receive a complaint about harassment and fail to act, they cannot plead

---

[59] Farkas, *et. al.* 2019.
[60] Farkas, *et. al.*, 2019.

ignorance and may be held liable if illegal conduct is found"[61]. The objectives of the training are to increase the awareness of the employees about sexual harassment and discrimination in the workplace so that they can readily identify such conduct if they observe it, to teach employees that they should step in and assist if they observe misconduct taking place, and that workers are adequately informed of the process for making complaints. Houseman (2019) also emphasizes that for training to be effective it must "actually make a difference in the office" by "molding employee perspectives" about proper versus improper workplace conduct, and thus "harassment training should not be used merely as a tool to avoid litigation" (p. 293). Accordingly, Houseman (2019) recommends the importance of "civility training" which teaches employees not only to recognize and report misconduct but "to treat each other with respect and humility" (p. 293). Similarly, the objectives of such a training program[62] are to design and build it around the concept of "human dignity in the workplace" as well as to focus on "the right to be safe, secure, and respected in the workplace" (pp. 117-118).

Specifically, regarding reporting procedures, colloquially known as "whistleblowing," it is incumbent on the employer to have a clear and definite whistleblowing policy and mechanism. Whistleblowing in the business context herein is the disclosure of wrongdoing by an employee of misconduct by his or her co-workers or by the company or organization itself. The #MeToo movement apparently has produced an effect on company whistleblowing. Brake (2019) asserts that "#MeToo has sparked a cultural reckoning with sexual harassment that

---

[61] Houseman, 2019, p. 445.
[62] Flores, 2019.

promises to spur more outspoken opposition to sexual harassment in the workplace" (p. 5). However, Brake (2019) adds that "as the #MeToo movement expands to push the boundaries of conventional understandings of sexual harms, retaliatory responses may become even more likely" (p. 2). A study found that one-third of the females surveyed indicated that they had been sexually harassed at work during their lifetimes, but that 71% never reported the harassment[63]. The EEOC Select Task Force study found that approximately three out of four employees who experienced harassment never even talked[64] to a manager, supervisor, or union representative regarding the harassing conduct. Moreover, employees who experienced harassment failed to report the harassing behavior or to file a complaint because they feared disbelief of their claim, inaction on their claim, blame, or social or professional retaliation. Another study indicated that only one out of four women who faced sexual harassment felt comfortable about coming forward with a complaint. Green (2019) explains that "pursuing a complaint of harassment constitutes a risky proposition. Approximately, 75 percent of those employees who do file formal complaints face some form of retaliation by their employers" (p. 128). Others warn that there may even be a "backlash" against the #MeToo movement and consequently that "blowing the whistle" on harassment at work may cause even more retaliation responses against female employees[65].

Consequently, regarding whistleblowing, we recommend a written and communicated reporting procedure that includes the following elements, to wit: a recitation of the

---

[63] Houseman, 2019, p. 282.
[64] Houseman, 2019, p. 293.
[65] Brake, 2019, p. 5.

specific steps necessary to start a harassment or discrimination complaint; a requirement that all employees must report all suspected occurrences of discrimination and harassment, including a statement that sanctions may be imposed for not reporting; a strong and clear prohibition of retaliation against the employee bringing the complaint or revealing the discrimination or harassment as well as a statement that any retaliation will be severely punished; and a statement that the process will remain confidential to the extent possible. Some[66] maintain that the complaint should initially be made to the employee's immediate supervisor; however, as per EEOC "suggestion," the employer should "designate at least one official outside the employee's chain of command to hear the complaint" if the employee does not feel comfortable in bringing the complaint to the immediate supervisor or feels it may be futile to do so. Regarding situations of sexual harassment, the authors further recommend that an employee who feels aggrieved by a manager, supervisor, or other employee preferring a paramour should be able to bring the situation to the attention of his or her manager, or, likewise, if the manager is a party romantically involved, to bring the matter to a leader above that manager or outside the aggrieved employee's hierarchal chain-of-command.

To conclude, reference again must be made to the federal district court in the aforementioned *Alatorre v. Mabus* case, where the court provided the following advice regarding anti-harassment policies and procedures: "The legal standard for evaluating an employer's efforts to prevent and correct harassment…is not whether any additional steps or measures would have been reasonable, if employed, but whether the

---

[66] Pearce and Lipin, 2015, pp. 350-51.

employer's actions, taken as a whole, established a reasonable mechanism for prevention and correction."[67] The basic policies and procedures recommended herein have been generally presented, but nonetheless they should go a long way in meeting the court's "reasonableness" standard, as well as combatting sexual harassment and discrimination in the workplace, and protecting both employers and employees. We now offer some specific recommendations regarding office romance policies, and especially on how to avoid any resulting sexual favoritism in the workplace.

Regulate Romantic Relationships

Legally, the general rule is that "office romance does not create a Title VII claim for those employees negatively affected by the relationship."[68] As one court explained, the fact that an office romance "touched on matters of sexuality" does not mean the conduct constituted a form of sex discrimination or created a hostile work environment[69]. Similarly, rumors or gossip of office romance as well as the failure to quell or suppress rumors are insufficient to support a hostile work environment lawsuit[70]. Nevertheless, promulgating policies on office romance and workplace dating is highly advisable. However, perhaps surprisingly, a survey conducted by the Society for Human Resource Management (SHRM) indicated that only 13% of 600 companies surveyed had a written policy addressing office romance[71]; and 14% stated they had an "unwritten" one.

---

[67] *Alatorre v. Mabus*, 2015, p. 25.
[68] *Delong v. Oklahoma*, 2016, p. 5.
[69] *Romero v. McCormick & Schmick Rest. Corp.*, 2020, p. 15.
[70] *Schneider v. GP Strategies Corp*, 2017.
[71] Morgan, 2010, p. 75.

Similarly, another Society for Human Resource Management survey revealed that only 36% of companies had a written policy on office romance[72] and 6% had a verbal policy.

All employers, therefore, should be proactive and accordingly have policies on relationships and dating among co-workers. Employers should also ensure that all the employees are aware of such policies. The policies must underscore to employees that there are appropriate legal as well as ethical standards of conduct at the workplace. The employees should also be advised that there may be career repercussions when they commence a relationship. For example, an employer can have a policy that when two employees in the same department start dating, one might need to be transferred to another department. The employees should be told in the office romance policy that before they embark on dating a colleague they should consider the potential problems and conflicts-of-interest that could arise, especially if they are working together on an important project and they then break up, since there could be adverse consequences for the project, team, and/or employer[73]. To avoid such a problem the policy could state that employees on the same project or work-team cannot date and form romantic relationships. In a more extreme policy, if the employees do decide to date, then one dating employee may have to resign or be discharged from the company. If one partner in a romantic relationship becomes a supervisor or manager then a similar sexual favoritism situation could arise. Accordingly, the subordinate employee should be transferred to another department or team. Until that time the manager must be told not to favor his or her partner in any way and that all

---

[72] Leong, 2019, p. 997.
[73] Workable.com., 2020; Cavico, Mujtaba, and Samuels, 2012.

members of the team must be treated in a fair and ethical manner. Also, if there is a breakup, perhaps caused by the subordinate employee, the manager or supervisor must be admonished not to discriminate or retaliate against his or her partner in any way. Professionalism and decorum in the workplace must be maintained; and consequently the former paramours must be warned that any "badmouthing," revelations of intimate details, or work sabotage will violate the company's Code of Ethics or Conduct and thus will subject the offender to disciplinary action[74].

At the very least, as emphasized, employers should very seriously consider policies that prohibit managers and supervisors from dating subordinate employees. Workable.com (2020) took a strict view on dating and thus recommended that a company prohibit managers and supervisors from dating team members or those who report to their team members, whether directly or indirectly. Moreover, it is recommended that those who are at a high level in the business hierarchy, for example, senior directors, should be forbidden from dating anyone who is below their level, regardless of whether they are in another department. However, managers who are below that high level, for example, a department head, should be allowed to have a dating relationship so long as their romantic partner is from another department or team and is at the same level or lower in the company hierarchy.

Another policy is to have managers and supervisors report dating type relationships; but not to require such reporting by lower-level employees. Of course, one must define "relationship" as to be very clear among all workers. Such a policy typically would not require the reporting of a "mere"

---

[74] Workable.com., 2020.

date[75]. As such, experts[76] emphasize that a basic Human Resource policy should be that the company will not be involved in the private lives of its employees; and thus the going out on a couple of dates or even a short term, for example, two month, relationship need not be reported to Human Resources; but if the relationship lasts longer Human Resources must be informed so as to better manage any perceptions of sexual favoritism, conflicts-of-interest, and office gossip. However, there is a "downside[77]" to any reporting requirement, and that is "some employees will violate this 'you must tell us' policy. Then, more serious problems can arise."

If the employer does establish a policy on office romance or dating in the workplace, the employer must ensure that all employees are aware of the policy and that the policy is consistently and fairly enforced[78]. At times these polices preclude employees dating clients, customers, suppliers, and distributors. There should be mandatory ground and/or online training to educate the employees as to the policy and to help ensure compliance. Office romance can fit into pre-existing training that many companies have pertaining to diversity, sensitivity, and of course sexual discrimination, harassment, and a hostile work environment. Nevertheless, restrictive dating polices may not be efficacious for a small business. A restrictive dating policy "is generally not practical in small business, especially one that employs family members. If the entrepreneur is employing her spouse, it is difficult for her to say that other employees cannot start dating"[79].

---

[75] Cavico, Mujtaba, and Samuels, 2012.
[76] Workable.com, 2020.
[77] Byun, 2014, p. 285.
[78] Davidson and Forsythe, 2011.
[79] Davidson and Forsythe, 2011, p. 186.

One proactive measure that employers can take to avoid liability for sexual harassment and discrimination as well as to avoid charges of sexual favoritism is called formally a "consensual relationship agreement," or more informally a "love contract"[80]. Some of the key features of the "love contract" are as follows[81]:

1. The romantically involved co-workers will state that their mutual love and affection is consensual and that their romance will neither interfere with their work responsibilities nor the workplace.
2. The contract is a written acknowledgment that the workplace romantic relationship between the employees is a consensual one. The contracts are voluntarily signed.
3. The intimate couple can disclose their relationship; also, most importantly for the employer, expressly state that their relationship is voluntary and consensual and that they will not engage in any inappropriate sexual or flirtatious conduct in the workplace.
4. "Love contracts" generally require the employees to obey all employment rules regarding office romance, including the company's policy on sexual discrimination and harassment.
5. The contracts can also be customized for specific situations. The love contract, for example, can require that the employees refrain from displays of affection at work and work-related functions and events, thereby mitigating any adverse effects based on sexual favoritism or perceived sexual favoritism.
6. The "love contract" can specifically and explicitly state that either romantically involved employee can terminate the relationship without fear of retribution and retaliation.
7. The "love contract" can state that the employees waive their rights to sue for sex discrimination and sexual

---

[80] Byun, 2014; Cavico, Mujtaba, and Samuels, 2012; Selvin, 2007.
[81] Byun, 2014, Cavico, Mujtaba, and Samuels, 2012; Morgan, 2010; Adams, 2009.

harassment for any actions or activities that occurred prior to or during the duration of the romantic engagement.

8. The contract also can state that each participant will seek arbitration rather than file sexual harassment lawsuits if the relationship ends.

9. The contract can state that each party to the workplace romance can end the relationship without fear of work-related retaliation.

10. The "love contract" can be used not only for senior executives, but also managers and supervisors as well as all romantically involved employees.

11. The contract typically will state that the romantically involved co-workers have read the company's sexual harassment policy, particularly those provisions dealing with the reporting of complaints and the firm admonition against retaliation; and, that they are free to end their romantic relationship without any adverse impact to their jobs.

12. The parties are to be given an opportunity to review the contract with an attorney first.

13. In the contract the parties must affirm that they were not coerced into signing the agreement, and that if any disputes arise under the agreement the matter will be subject to arbitration.

14. The signed original "love contract" is usually filed with the company's Human Resources department.

A "love contract," therefore, can help protect the employer from discrimination, harassment, and retaliation claims, particularly favoritism-based ones, as well as help educate the employees as to workplace rules and standards of conduct, and to ensure that the employees' romantic relationship does not interfere with their job performance or the performance of their co-workers. Morgan (2010) calls these contracts "the office version of a pre-nup," but seems to rue the fact that "such documentation effectively takes the fun out of an office romance"; and perhaps "that's the point" (p. 75). However, the "love contract" should bring the romantic relationship "to the surface," where it can be dealt with in the workplace in a rational and mutually satisfactory manner, as opposed to an outright ban on workplace romance, which might force the romantically involved workers to "go underground" with their romance, thereby inhibiting their work performance. One-sided or unrequited love is always problematic; yet whether a "love contract" is *the* solution is still a matter of debate.

Even though the employer may have the right to establish and enforce such a no-dating policy, and concomitantly to discharge employees for violating the policy, any inconsistent and/or selective enforcement of the policy may engender discrimination lawsuits by adversely affected "protected" employees pursuant to Civil Rights statutes. Similarly, if an employer gets too intrusive in enforcing such a policy, for example, by monitoring and surveillance, the employer may risk a lawsuit for the intentional tort of invasion of privacy, thereby subjecting the employer to liability. Kreis (2020) emphasizes that in any situation a "cardinal caveat" of office romance policy and practice is that "former relationships do not provide jilted lovers *carte blanche* to engage in sex discrimination against former partners" (p. 190) and, the authors add, to engage in sexual harassment or any form of bullying, workplace mobbing, demeaning, or abusive conduct.

There are a wide variety of office romance policies. Some companies, such as IBM and Xerox, have formal policies that allow relationships between employees who are not on the same management hierarchical chain. Other employers, like Google and Facebook, have policies that limit employees to a single romantic overture to a co-worker, and if the co-worker turns the employee's request down, or even if he or she responds ambiguously, for example, by saying "I'm busy," no further requests can be made[82]. As such, Leong (2019) notes that "many companies have begun to develop more assertive policies in the wake of the revelations from #MeToo" (p. 999). If an employee continues to ask for dates, engages in unwanted flirting, and becomes annoying or even threatening, the aggrieved employee should first ask him or her to stop the conduct, but if it continues the aggrieved employee should inform his or her manager and Human Resources[83].

An example of a more prohibitive office romance policy involves the firm Blackrock, which is the world's largest money manager. In the past, the company instructed its employees that they had to notify Human Resources anytime they had a romantic relationship with another employee. However, the company updated its office romance policy, and the employees must also disclose relationships with employees of the company's service providers, vendors, clients, and other third parties if the non-Blackrock employee is within a group or team that interacts with Blackrock[84]. Such a policy has been deemed "overboard" by one commentator who worries about the burden it will put on the company's Human Resources department to make judgements when one of the company's (many) employees goes on a date, as well as the burden it will put on an individual employee who now must ascertain if the person, he or she wants to date has any connection with Blackrock[85]. The company, nonetheless, defends its expanded policy with its

---

[82] Green, 2019; Leong, 2019.
[83] Workable.com, 2020.
[84] Gasparino, 2020.
[85] Gasparino, 2020, p. 49.

inclusion of inter-team relationships by asserting that the policy prevents conflicts-of-interest and favoritism and makes life easier for the employees as an assessment of whether dating that is permissible is now in the hands of the Human Resources department and not the employees[86]. However, even if companies such as Blackrock, are instituting more restrictive office romance policies, perhaps in response to the #MeToo movement, nonetheless office romance will never[87] die.

Yet, regardless of the legal, ethical, and practical challenges attendant to office romance, some employers today, especially those with many young workers, have taken a more neutral position on office romance and thus have office romance policies that allow dating among co-workers. For example, Cisco Systems, whose dating policy states that the company "does not encourage or discourage consensual relationships in the workplace." However, the policy also says that relationships between supervisors and subordinate employees are "frowned upon," and may result in a transfer or reassignment[88]. Another example is Southwest Airlines, which at one point employed over 1000 married couples, and explicitly allowed consensual office romance relationships. However, the airline has a policy and a process that affords an employee who objects to a particular office romance to complain to the Human Resources department or to a manager, who, in turn, is responsible for finding a remedy if the office romance negatively impacts the company's "culture."

The primary objective of these restrictive policies and measures is to shield employers from liability pursuant to

---

[86] Gasparino, 2020.
[87] Zillman, 2018.
[88] Shellenbarger, 2010, pp. D1.

sexual harassment and sexual discrimination laws if the office romance later degenerates into a workplace dispute. Presumably, the romance was commenced by the employees based on their own free will without any claim of coercion or intimidation for sex, which of course is the genesis of many sexual harassment lawsuits. Employers also want to minimize morale problems at work, especially charges of sexual favoritism, and the concomitant disruption, as well as negative publicity – externally as well as internally, which can all affect the bottom-line of the business. Furthermore, an executive's failed office romance may impair the executive's ability to lead the company. To complicate matters further from a practical vantage point, the employee having the romantic relationship with a senior level executive may perceive that due to the relationship with the executive he or she may think he or she has, or will be perceived as having, more power and influence beyond his or her official job status and authority. Employers thus want to take steps to not only avoid legal liability, but also to ensure that office romances do not hinder job performance. The productivity and teamwork adversely affected may not only involve the romantically involved employees but also their co-workers. Accusations of conflict-of-interest, whether real or perceived, have the potential to disrupt and negatively impact the workplace. Damage to the value of merit as a core principle for promotion can be another very negative consequence. Office romances can be a major distraction at work, even without charges of favoritism and conflict-of-interest.

Nevertheless, it is difficult to have an effective total ban on dating since human nature and sexual attraction will likely overcome any employer policy. People will still get romantically involved at the workplace regardless of any policy. People meet other people most frequently at work. Total prohibitions of relationships may drive them "underground." "Turning a blind eye" means that the employer has lost an opportunity to provide guidelines and to counsel the dating couple. Of course, dating employees may attempt to keep their relationship secret; yet secrecy can be difficult to achieve in certain workplaces, particularly where the corporate culture is one of openness and informality and where the employees work long hours together. Furthermore, the relationship is likely to come into the open anyway, but co-workers may feel they have been lied to and thus the trust among the employees could be eroded[89].

Consequently, employees who date and form relationships, whether secretly or openly, should be very scrupulous about keeping aspects of their romantic relationship out of the office. They first should familiarize themselves with the company's policy on office dating and romance. Employees who commence dating also should be aware of the risks involved, such as perceptions of preferential treatment or sexual favoritism, conflicts-of-interest, whether real or perceived, and the risk of harm to reputations. Moreover, researchers have noted that there is additional effort that dating co-workers go to in order to prevent "fallout" from their office romance[90]. For example, some dating co-workers can ask to be assigned to different departments, teams, or projects. In addition to informing management, some couples inform their co-workers, including new employees, they are dating. They also can tell newly hired employees that if they felt uncomfortable about their dating, they should inform a manager. Romantically

---

[89] Gallo, 2019.
[90] Shellenbarger, 2010, p. D1.

involved employees also can tell newly hired employees that if they felt uncomfortable about their dating relationship, they should inform them as well as a manager.

The romantically involved co-workers should avoid any public displays of affection or flirting; rather, they should act as professional colleagues at all times; otherwise, their co-workers may feel very uncomfortable. The romantically involved couple surely should avoid calling one's co-worker whom one is dating "Honey" or similar words of affection, as well as avoiding public displays of affection. The romantically involved employees should thus avoid the following actions: excessively communicating with each other in person or by emails, messages, and calls; arguing with each other (i.e., "lovers' quarrels"); kissing, inappropriate touching, and discussing or boasting about the relationship in the workplace; as well as avoiding other public displays of affection[91]. However, the following types of conduct should be deemed permissible: passing by one romantic partner's office, stopping by, and chatting for a short time; discussing joint plans, e.g., vacation, during meals or breaks; and coming to and leaving from work together[92]. Breakups may be painful; and telling one's co-workers about the breakup may be awkward, but co-workers who have been told of the relationship should also be informed of its ending[93].

Yet because of the laws against sexual harassment and discrimination as well as the problems attendant to office romance, especially sexual favoritism in the workplace, some employers strictly forbid any type of dating; whereas others

---

[91] Workable.com., 2020; Shellenbarger, 2010.
[92] Workable.com., 2020.
[93] Gallo, 2019.

permit it but only if the employees are in different divisions or departments; others permit it but require employees to declare their relationship and, as noted, sign some type of dating contract stating that the relationship is a consensual one and also allowing the employer to separate the dating co-workers at work. Clearly, to avoid legal problems as well as charges of sexual favoritism, it is recommended that an office romance policy should forbid a manager or supervisor dating a subordinate employee because of the inequality of the relationship, the potential for preferential treatment, and the potential for legal liability for sexual harassment on the part of the employer[94]. Gallo (2019) explains that regarding managers and supervisors dating subordinates: "This is where conflicts of interests are most stark. It's hard to be objective when giving someone you're dating a performance review, for example. And you don't want people to think that you're being unduly favored; it can erode your own confidence and hurt the team's morale" (p. 3). Therefore, if a manager or supervisor and a subordinate employee do embark on a romantic relationship it is advisable that either one or both should be asked to transfer to a different division or department or perhaps leave his or her job[95]. Moreover, the company policy should forbid a manager or supervisor from hiring his or her spouse, partner, or paramour for the department or team; but if so, one of them should transfer to another department or team or quit.

The office romance policy and training must emphasize that employees who are in romantic relationships need to conduct themselves in a proper and professional manner in the

---

[94] Workable.com., 2020; Gallo, 2019; Byun, 2014; Cavico, Mujtaba, and Samuels, 2012.
[95] Byun, 2014.

workplace. Any policy or training should be "Focusing[96] on what is appropriate behavior, and how it might impact the office environment and working relationships within that environment." Consequently, any public displays of love and affection in the workplace, as well as gratitude to a partner, though perhaps at times tempting, must be forbidden, because such conduct will make the other employees, as well as customers and clients, feel awkward and uncomfortable, thereby impeding efficiency, effectiveness, and productivity in the workplace, as well as creating an atmosphere that is sexually offensive and thus illegal.

In summary, we can say that, at work the employees should be focused on their responsibilities as employees and not on romance. Moreover, even if a company does not have an office romance prohibition, the affected employees should first be aware if the relationship is adversely affecting their own job performance and productivity. The parties should also raise the issue with Human Resources as well as consider transferring to a different division or department of the company to avoid any perceptions of sexual favoritism and conflict-of-interest. Office romance, regardless of how much one disapproves of the practice, cannot really be stamped out, as adults who are sexually and romantically attracted to one another will "find a way," but the practice can, and should be, regulated and moderated in a legal, ethical, fair, and balanced manner. It is the primary responsibility of the business leaders, human resources professionals, and managers to achieve these core values in a practical and functional manner for the firm.

---

[96] Mainiero and Jones, 2013a, p. 377.

6

Non-Disclosure Agreements

This section focuses on non-disclosure agreements (NDAs) as they relate to employment, office romance, sexual favoritism, and sexual harassment issues. The chapter will define and explain NDAs, analyze them from legal and ethical perspectives, and provide suitable recommendations to employers and managers as to the use of NDAs in sexual harassment cases.

Definition and Explanation of NDAs

Simply and generally stated, a *non-disclosure agreement* is a contractual agreement, typically arising out of the settlement of a lawsuit, in which the parties – the employer and employee in the context herein – agree that in consideration for a payment by the employer to the employee, the employee as well as the employer promise not to communicate the particulars of the lawsuit on settlement negotiations, discuss the NDA's terms, and even in some cases to refer to the NDA. Moreover, if an NDA is a "draconian" one, it will not only prevent the employee from saying anything about the dispute at hand, but also prevent the employee from participating in any other legal action against the employer[97]. NDAs are commonly found in employment contracts. Companies rely on NDAs to protect trade secrets and other confidential information, but also as part of the settlement of lawsuits, including for the purposes herein of sexual harassment lawsuits. Penalties for violating the NDA can be harsh, ranging from the employee paying back the entire settlement money received to additional monetary losses that the employer suffered due to the employee's breach of the agreement, including damages to the employer's reputation and attorneys' fees.

Today, however, there is growing societal and legal concern that these agreements are fundamentally wrong because they have prevented the victims of sexual harassment and sexual assault from speaking out, and have had the perverse result of protecting serial sexual predators and abusers. Moreover, with the advent of the #MeToo movement and the spotlight #MeToo has been focusing on high-profile sexual harassment cases, there appears to be occurring a marked change in the use of NDAs in sexual harassment cases. These changes have been caused by recent changing societal norms, legal pronouncements, moral pressure, as well as the practical concerns of employers and managers.

Legal Analysis

In this legal section the authors will examine the changing legal landscape for NDAs with reference to federal law, state law, as well as the common law "public policy" doctrine.

First, as a direct result of the #MeToo movement, many states have by statute recently prohibited or limited the use of

---

[97] Spiggle, 2020, p. 2.

NDAs in sexual harassment as well as discrimination cases. For example, the New York law enacted in 2018 requires that the NDA be the choice of the employee if the NDA is part of a settlement agreement that involves sexual harassment allegations. The New York law also gives the employee 21 days to consider the terms of the NDA and seven days to revoke it. Moreover, in 2019, New York expanded the law to encompass all types of harassment and not just sexual harassment[98]. California, New Jersey, and Nevada also prohibit NDAs in resolving sexual harassment claims; and other states that restricted their use include Arizona, Illinois, Maryland, Oregon, Tennessee, Vermont, Virginia, and Washington state. The California law which prohibits NDAs in employment contracts is called the STAND Act, which means Stand Together Against Non-Disclosures Act[99]. The 2019 New Jersey law not only forbids NDAs in cases of sexual harassment but all types of harassment, discrimination, and retaliation against protected parties. Pennsylvania was considering legislation to limit the use of NDAs in workplace sexual harassment and discrimination cases[100] as was Massachusetts[101].

These statutes vary, of course; but generally, these state statutes operate to make NDAs unenforceable if they prevent the disclosure of information regarding sexual harassment or sexual assaults. Some statutes have had exceptions, for example allowing the victim to request confidentiality, or permitting the parties to keep confidential the terms of the settlement, the monetary nature and amount of the settlement, and/or the fact

---

[98] Haigh and Wirtz, 2020; Huang, 2019.
[99] Levey, 2019.
[100] Call, 2018.
[101] Smith-Lee, 2020.

that a settlement exists[102]. These preceding "exceptions," of course, do not affect the main prohibition in the law that nullifies any agreement not to disclose the underlying nature of the harassment allegations[103]. These state laws obviously will affect the way settlement agreements are drafted and applied in the relevant jurisdiction, yet not just in the states that have jurisdiction over the workplace dispute and settlement agreement, but other employers in other states who perhaps can discern legally "which way the wind is blowing."

On the federal level, in 2017, due to the major tax law changes in the Federal Tax Cut and Jobs Act, companies are now prohibited from deducting the payment and expenses of settlements relating to sexual harassment and discrimination, including attorneys' fees and litigation costs[104]. Also, on the federal level, there is a bill in Congress, called the Sunlight in Workplace Harassment Act, which though not directly prohibiting the use of NDAs in sexual harassment cases, would require publicly traded companies to provide information regarding settlements of disputes involving harassment and/or discrimination pursuant to federal employment discrimination and harassment laws[105]. As of the writing of this book, the bill has been referred to the Senate Committee[106] on Banking, Housing, and Urban Affairs, but has not yet been promulgated into law. The federal courts also have ruled that an NDA will not prevent an employee from reporting sexual harassment or discrimination as well as retaliation to the Equal Employment Opportunity Commission (EEOC) or for participating in an

---

[102] Haigh and Wirtz, 2020; Tippett, 2019.
[103] Haigh and Wirtz, 2020.
[104] Smith-Lee, 2020; Haigh and Wirtz, 2020; Huang, 2019.
[105] Huang, 2019.
[106] Congress.Gov, 2022.

EEOC investigation or proceeding[107]. Moreover, the NDA cannot prohibit an employee from reporting a criminal act, such as sexual assault, to law enforcement authorities[108]. Of course, sexual harassment, for example by words, may not rise to the level of an "assault"; and, also, an adversely affected employee may not comprehend that the NDA does not prohibit reporting the crime to the police.

Moreover, there is also on the federal level a bill in Congress, the *EMPOWER Act*, which means Ending the Monopoly of Power Over Workplace Harassment Through Education and Reporting, which would forbid employers from requiring employees to sign non-disclosure agreements as a condition of employment[109]. However, there is an exception in the statute which allows NDAs in settlement or separation agreements if they are made after a claim for sexual harassment is instituted, the NDAs are mutually agreed upon by the employer and employee, and they mutually benefit both parties. This settlement exception is so broad that Levy (2019) warns that the exception "might ultimately swallow the rule and negate the purposes of the law" (p. 4). Thus far during the final publication process of this book, in March 2022, the federal bill has been referred to several committees in the U.S. House of Representatives but has not yet been promulgated into law.

On the state level, in addition, the courts in several states, using the common law, have ruled that such a prohibition in a contractual agreement is void as against the "public policy" of a jurisdiction, which doctrine protects actions that promote the health, safety, and welfare of the people of a state as well as

---

[107] Levy, 2019.
[108] Taylor & Ring, 2020.
[109] Levy, 2019.

actions that support the administration of the criminal justice system[110]. Accordingly, courts have ruled that NDAs are inimical to the public good, are oppressive and immoral, hinder the administration of justice, and thus are illegal and void under public policy doctrine rationales.

To conclude, since the U.S. is a federal system with federal, that is, national, law, as well as the law of its constituent elements – states – an aggrieved party in addition to any federal law must naturally refer to the state law in his or her relevant jurisdiction to see if an NDA is prohibited or limited in sexual harassment as well as discrimination cases. Regardless of legality it is also necessary to determine if ethically NDAs are moral in sexual harassment cases.

Ethical Analysis

Accordingly, the authors will now examine NDAs in sexual harassment cases from the aforementioned four major ethical theories – Ethical Egoism, Ethical Relativism, Utilitarianism, and Kantian ethics. As always pursuant to ethical analysis we will attempt to discern the moral course of action regarding the use of NDAs in sexual harassment cases in the workplace.

First, pursuant to Ethical Egoism, granted an NDA as part of a settlement agreement will (initially at least) keep instances of sexual harassment hidden, as well as save the employer the time, cost, and effort, and concomitant bad publicity of a trial. Yet if the employer attempts to enforce the NDA, assuming, of course, that it is even enforceable, there is going to be a civil trial anyway, which is a matter of public record, thereby obviating the protective efficacy of the NDA.

---

[110] Taylor & Ring, 2020

Moreover, the fact that the employer has the NDA, and then attempts to enforce it, would typically result in a crescendo of bad publicity, criticism, reputational loss, especially if the perpetrators are high-profile wrongdoers and/or the circumstances are painful and lurid and the amount paid for the victim's silence is not commensurate with her/his harm. Litigation of an NDA is not only a legal, economic, and public relations "hassle" for the employer, and thus it can open a "Pandora's box" for the employer[111]. Consequently, based on egoistic concerns brought about and heightened by legal and moral pressure, as well as "selfish" practical concerns, some companies, such as PepsiCo and Conde Nast, no longer use NDAs in settling sexual harassment and discrimination lawsuits. PepsiCo still uses NDAs and confidentiality agreements for other matters, for example, prohibiting the disclosure of trade secrets and other confidential information. Yet the company explicitly informs its employees that the NDA does not limit their right to speak out regarding allegations of sexual harassment, discrimination, or retaliation[112].

Pursuant to Ethical Relativism, the astute observer can sense a shift in attitudes regarding the use of NDAs in sexual harassment as well as discrimination cases. Societal concern in particular has been focused on the use of NDAs, especially in high-profile cases – business, entertainment, and political – to hide and suppress negative information about sexual harassment and even more seriously sexual assault in the workplace. Haigh and Wirtz (2020) maintain that "public opinion seems to be that NDAs should be abolished, or at least used far less often. And public and internal pressure from

---

[111] Spiggle, 2020, p. 5.
[112] Safdar, 2020.

employees is proving effective…. (A) titan in the publishing world has just promised publicly that it will not require NDAs as part of the settlement of matters involving discrimination or harassment. Other employers will likely follow as pressure from the public, and employees, continues to build" (p. 1).

Pursuant to Utilitarianism, one can initially perceive certain positive consequences for both employers and employees. NDAs can facilitate the settlement of a lawsuit. As such, the employer saves the time, money, and effort of litigation as well as the prevention of negative publicity; whereas the employee gives up the right to file a lawsuit, gets paid a sum of money as compensation, and thus avoids having to pursue the lawsuit, with all the attendant time, cost, stress, and since typically a public trial the possible embarrassment, and, moreover, a lawsuit that the plaintiff employee could in fact lose.

However, societal mores and the laws regarding NDAs are rapidly changing, so first the employer must be sure that the NDA is even legal in a sexual harassment case in its pertinent jurisdiction. In addition, the astute employer also has to consider whether it would be even worthwhile to attempt to enforce the legal NDA; that is, is the employer prepared for any negative consequences, such as negative publicity, moral pressure, criticism and perhaps condemnation, and even maybe threats of boycotts; also, is the employer prepared to defend the circumstances and terms of the NDA in a public forum as well internally among its own employees? Moreover, from a broader societal perspective, the NDA by silencing victims of sexual harassment and sexual assault keeps hidden wrongful behavior, thereby allowing this unlawful behavior to continue unabated, and in some situations for many years, as was the case in several high-profile business and entertainment cases. The NDA impedes free speech, which a democratic society cherishes; and in the sexual harassment context herein protects rich, powerful, well-connected, serial sexual predators and abusers, which one certainly would think our society condemns and thus wants to punish and deter. Accordingly, in the opinion of authors, there are more bad consequences than good that can emanate from the NDA in a sexual harassment situation; and thus, NDAs are immoral under Utilitarian ethical analysis.

Pursuant to Kantian ethics, the authors contend that it is demeaning and disrespectful to the aggrieved employee who is under a great deal of pressure to settle a sexually "charged" and potentially very embarrassing workplace harassment situation to silence him or her from speaking of the situation. Moreover, it is demeaning and disrespectful to other employees, including future employees, by forbidding the victimized employee to speak out, since such silence will allow the sexual harasser or predator to continue with the wrongful conduct. Furthermore, society is demeaned and disrespected since the wrongful conduct very well could include criminal conduct in the form of sexual assault which obviously society wants to punish and deter. There is also a school of thought that says that attorneys are acting unethically for even requesting NDAs in sexual harassment and other cases since these attorneys are in essence committing obstruction of justice[113].

Therefore, since NDAs in sexual harassment cases are against the true self-interest of the employer they are immoral pursuant to Ethical Egoism; since they are contrary to societal norms, they are immoral pursuant under Ethical Relativism; since they are inimical to the general welfare and the public

---

[113] Tippett, 2019.

good, they are immoral under Utilitarianism; and since they are demeaning and respectful to the victim and potential future victims they are immoral under Kantian ethics.

Recommendations

Consequently, even in a state that allows NDAs in sexual harassment cases, the ethically egoistic employer should think "long and hard" about utilizing such agreements. Primarily based on the publicity and moral pressures caused by the #MeToo movement, societal mores are clearly changing, and the laws are rapidly following suit. The "selfish" employer has to consider two key questions: first, even if there is an NDA is it worth the negative publicity to even try to enforce the agreement; and second, if so, would the employer feel comfortable defending the terms of the NDA in the "court of public opinion."[114]

Therefore, the authors would counsel employers that based on legal, ethical, and practical concerns, employers and managers should abjure the use of NDAs in sexual assault and harassment as well as in discrimination cases. However, the employer should always grant the victim the right to request confidentiality, and formally so too by means of a contractual agreement initiated by the employee. NDAs, of course, still can and should be used, and properly so, to protect conventional, confidential business information like trade secrets, customer/client lists, and business plans and strategies. Of course, the true solution to the NDA question is for the employer to create a positive business culture based on the values of legality, morality, fairness, respect, diversity, and inclusion, thereby obviating harassment and discrimination in the workplace. It is the important task of business leaders,

---

[114] Tippett, 2019.

managers, and human resources professionals to ensure that such a just, values-based workplace exists.

7

Values and Business Leadership

Values possess worth. Therefore, it is important for business leaders, managers, and human resource professionals to embody a values-based organizational culture and decision-making processes as they attempt to adapt, innovate, influence, manage, lead, and transform workplace romance policies that are legal, ethical, inclusive, and sustainable over time. This book has examined the values of legality, morality, and practicality in the context of the laws against sexual harassment and discrimination in the workplace and the legal, ethical, and practical challenges of workplace romance and sexual favoritism. Leaders must be keenly aware of these values and their application. Leadership, therefore, is an important topic for business leaders in our society and for students as our potential leaders in business and the professions. The leader must "know the way, show the way, and go the way (lead)."

Self-awareness is a critical feature of leadership, that is, being cognizant of your own situation as well as the impact of your actions on other stakeholders of the company. A leader may need to apply new and varied approaches, ideas, solutions, and techniques to solve problem, especially with the very problematic issues of office romance and sexual favoritism. A leader must also be aware of *"blind spots"* – personally and for his or her organization; that is, the leader must be aware of weaknesses related to what is not being done well or what is not being done at all. Yet, the leader must know his or her and the company's strengths; and the leader should also be able to identify opportunities. Most importantly, the leader must not be "blind-sided" by weaknesses (e.g., being accused of acting illegally or being accused of acting immorally though acting legally). However, a person as well as a business entity may have hidden strengths, which the leader must become aware of, bring to light, and highlight.

Business leaders, of course are expected to make sound business decisions and thus achieve excellence in results; also, they must be proactive; that is, the leader must be a "shaper" not a mere "reactor": The leader must anticipate challenges, thereby knowing the way, showing the way to solving them, and leading the way to implementing relevant solutions. The subject matters of workplace romance and sexual favoritism cry out for such proactive and efficacious business leadership. Moreover, it is of critical importance for the leader to embrace and demonstrate legal and moral behavior and to establish an organizational culture of morality and ethics that is inclusive and sustainable. Such an appropriate culture is essential when it comes to eliminating sexual harassment and discrimination and sexual favoritism in the workplace.

Local norms and organizational cultures across nations can make a difference in what is accepted and practiced. Of course, it should be noted that what works in one organization or country cannot and should not always be duplicated verbatim as some national practices and cultures may not be a good fit for it. As reported by experts[115] in international management, Walmart employees often engage in the *"Walmart cheer"* to start their day and that this is a way for them to show inclusivity and express their pride in the company through the local language of each country. Despite Walmart's multinational success with their cheer, some of its internal practices proved to be less than satisfactory to the German market. Their brochure which outlined the workplace code of ethics was translated from English to German without considering the local interpretations, and the message was not expressed the way Walmart had intended. Supposedly, it warned employees of potential supervisor-employee relationships, implying that it can lead to cases of sexual harassment, and encouraged reports of "improper behavior" to managers and company officials. The average German interpreted this to mean that there was a total ban on any romantic workplace relationships and saw the reporting methods as more of snitching on or betraying co-workers through legal matters instead of seeing this to benefit the company. So, the Walmart organizational culture and written policy on workplace romance did not translate well into the German language and culture; as such, these types of policies should be localized with proper language and intention.

The societal expectations today are that businesses will act not "only" legally to prevent any form of inequity and harassment, but also morally. As such, business is expected to have a positive and sustainable impact on all its stakeholders, including society as a whole. Therefore, the responsibilities of business leaders today are that they must in the leadership of their firms first obey the law and then go "above and beyond" the law to conduct business in a moral manner. The leader also

---

[115] Luthans and Doh, 2021.

must be prepared for difficult issues and challenges, such as the ones addressed in this book. Accordingly, the business leader must be concerned with not only the practical and economic aspects of the business but with its legal and moral conduct.

8

Conclusion

Sexual conduct in the workplace has been highlighted in recent years with the onset of the #MeToo movement which has imparted a greater awareness of improper sexual conduct in the workplace as well as empowered victims and other employees to disclose such wrongdoing. Therefore, the authors sought to examine the important topics of sexual favoritism and office romance in the workplace from practical, legal, and ethical perspectives. Accordingly, after the introductory and background section, this book addressed the laws regarding sexual favoritism in the workplace.

The three main legal areas – the general rule of isolated instances of sexual favoritism, the *quid pro quo* exception, and the hostile environment exception – were explained and illustrated. The legal versus the moral dichotomy of the general rule of sexual favoritism was underscored.

As authors, we tried to emphasize that there should be relevant HR policies around workplace romance to prevent any sexual harassment issues. Furthermore, another best practice that managers and organizations should follow regarding workplace romance is having an appropriate dating policy in place that is communicated to all employees. The Society for Human Resource Management[116] (SHRM) provides a clear boundary between business interactions and personal socialization in the workplace. The procedures outlined in the dating policy by SHRM include the following:

    (a) All employees must conduct themselves in an appropriate manner during working hours so that they do not hinder productivity.

    (b) Prohibit employees from engaging in inappropriate physical contact on work premises.

    (c) Employees must disclose relationships among supervisors, managers, or executives for the company to determine any potential conflicts of interest.

    (d) When romantic relationships are reported, there can be reallocation of duties, including termination, demotions, performance appraisals, promotions and/or compensation to resolve a conflict of interest.

    (e) Referrals should be made to the director of HR for any concerns regarding the employee dating policy ("Employee dating policy", n.d.).

So, a clearly defined dating policy can limit claims of favoritism, uncomfortable work environments such as a hostile workplace, and avoid obvious conflicts of interest.

The book then addressed some of the legal aspects of office romance, particularly how office romance can engender sexual favoritism and then sexual harassment and discrimination in the workplace. Next, the authors analyzed the topics of sexual favoritism and office romance from an ethical perspective to determine the morality of certain workplace policies and conducts. Four ethical theories were applied to

---

[116] SHRM - "Employee dating policy", 2021.

make moral conclusions, to wit: Ethical Egoism, Ethical Relativism, Utilitarianism, and Kantian ethics.

The positive and negative consequences of office romance were set forth in a balanced manner. Then, based on the legal and ethical analysis, the authors made several practical recommendations for management, first, generally, to avoid lawsuits for sexual harassment and discrimination and to curtail sexual favoritism, and then specifically regarding appropriate workplace romance policies and procedures, with particular attention on the so-called "love contract." The authors also discussed the related and important topic of non-disclosure agreements (NDAs) in sexual harassment cases, which subject has been brought into sharp focus by means of the #MeToo movement. Legal and ethical analyses of the subject were provided; and the authors made suitable recommendations as to the use of NDAs in sexual harassment cases. The authors concluded their book by a discussion of values and business leadership in the context of sexual favoritism and workplace romance.

The goal of the authors in this book was, and is, to help employers and managers to attain a workplace that is practical, effective, functional, and efficacious, but also one that is legal, fair, ethical, moral, inclusive, and just. The authors trust that they have achieved these goals in a readable, intellectually stimulating, and helpful manner and that you, the readers, have enjoyed their work.

9

References

Adams, Susan (2009). How to Have a Successful Office Romance. *Forbes.com*. Retrieved from: http://www.forbes.com/2009/08/11/office-romance-affair-leadership-career-sex.html.

Alatorre v. Mabus, 2015 U.S. Dist. LEXIS 60850 (District Court for the Southern District of California 2015).

Avendaño, A. (2018). Sexual Harassment in the Workplace: Where Were the Unions? *Labor Studies Journal*, *43*(4), 245-262.

Binion v. PNC Bank, Nat'l Ass'n, 2017 U.S. Dist. LEXIS 36867 (District Court for the Northern District of Alabama 2017).

Blount v. Northrop Grumman Info. Tech Overseas, Inc., 2014 U.S. Dist. LEXIS 146407 (District Court for the Eastern District of Virginia 2014).

Brake, Deborah L. (Fall 2019). Coworker Retaliation in the #MeToo Era. *University of Baltimore Law Review*, 49, pp. 1-58.

Broderick v. Ruder, 685 F. Supp. 1269 (District for the District of Columbia 1988).

Byun, Kibum (Fall 2014). You Can Get Fired for Flirting: Critique of Sex Discrimination Law in the Workplace Through Nelson v. Knight. *Cardozo Journal of Law & Gender*, 21, pp. 259-287.

Call, Keith A. (2018). #MeToo Movement and the Impact on Non-Disclosure Agreements. *SCM News and Opinions*. Retrieved 10/31/20 from: scmlaw.com/metoo-movement-and-the-impact-on-non-disclosure-agreements.

Cavico, F. J. and Mujtaba, B. G. (2021). Workplace Romance and Sexual Favoritism in the #MeToo Workplace: Legal and Practical Considerations for Management. *Equality, Diversity and Inclusion*, 40(6), 667-689.

Cavico, Frank J. and Mujtaba, Bahaudin G. (2021). *Common Law Torts in Business and How to Avoid Them: A Handbook for Managers.* Davie, Florida: ILEAD Academy, LLC.

Cavico, F. J. and Mujtaba, B. G. (2020). *Business Law for the Entrepreneur and Manager (4th edition).* ILEAD Academy: Florida.

Cavico, F.J. and Mujtaba, B.G. (2018). Teaching Law, Ethics, and Social Responsibility in a School of Business: A Value-Driven Approach to Leadership and Sustainability. *Marketing and Management Innovations,* 4, pp. 263-81.

Cavico, F. J. and Mujtaba, B. G. (2016). *Developing a Legal, Ethical, and Socially Responsible Mindset for Sustainable Leadership.* ILEAD Academy: Florida.

Cavico, F.J. and Mujtaba, B.G. (2014). *Legal Challenges for the Global Manager and Entrepreneur* (2nd Edition). Dubuque, Iowa: Kendall Hunt Publishing Company.

Cavico, F.J. and Mujtaba, B.G. (2013). *Business Ethics: The Moral Foundation of Effective Leadership, Management, and Entrepreneurship* (3rd Edition). Boston, Massachusetts: Pearson Publishing Company.

Cavico, F.J., Mujtaba, B.G., Petrescu, M., and Muffler. S. (2015). "A Kiss is but a Kiss": Cultural Mores, Ethical Relativism, and Sexual Harassment Liability. *Open Law and Ethics Journal,* 1, 38-50.

Cavico, F.J., Muffler, S.C., and Mujtaba, B.J. (2012). Sexual Orientation and Gender Identity in the American Workplace: Legal and Ethical Considerations. *International Journal of Humanities and Social Sciences,* 2(1), 1-20.

Cavico, F.J., Mujtaba, B.G., and Samuels, M. (2012). Office Romance: Legal Challenges and Strategic Implications. *International Journal of Management, IT, and Engineering,* 2(8), 10-35.

Chory, R. M., & Hoke, H. G. G. (2019). Young love at work: Perceived effects of workplace romance among millennial generation organizational members. *The Journal of psychology, 153*(6), 575-598.

Cofer v. Parker-Hannifin Corp., 194 F. Supp. 3d 1014 (District Court for the Southern District of California 2016).

Congress.Gov., H.R.1521 – EMPOWER ACT. Retrieved February 17, 2022 from: https://www.congress.gov/bill/116th-congress/house-bill/1521.

Congress.Gov., S, 2454 – Sunlight in Workplace Harassment Act. Retrieved February 17, 2022, from: https:///www.congress.gov/bill/115th-congress/senate-bill/2454.

Crisanto v. Cnty. Tulare, 2015 U.S. Dist. LEXIS 154734 (District Court for the Eastern District of California 2015).

Davidson, David D. and Forsythe, Lynn M. (2011). *The Entrepreneur's Legal Companion*. Boston, Massachusetts: Prentice Hall.

DeCinto v. Westchester County Medical Center, 807 F.2d 304(Second Circuit Court of Appeals1986), *certiorari denied*, 108 Sup. Ct. 89 (1987).

DeLong v. Oklahoma, 2016 U.S. Dist. LEXIS 56410 (District Court for the Western District of Oklahoma 2016).

Dobrich, W., Dranoff, S., and Maatman, G. (2002). *The Manager's Guide to Preventing a Hostile Work Environment.* McGraw-Hill: New York.

Doyle v. Advanced Fraud Sols., LLC, 2020 U.S. Dist. LEXIS 46642(District Court for the Middle District of North Carolina 2020).

Elsesser, K. (2019). These 6 Surprising Office Romance Stats Should Be A Wake-Up Call For Organizations. Forbes. Retrieved from: https://www.forbes.com/sites/kimelsesser/2019/02/14/these-6-surprising-office-romance-stats-should-be-a-wake-up-call-to-organizations/?sh=245b7dc323a2

Employee dating policy. (2021). SHRM. Retrieved from: https://www.shrm.org/resourcesandtools/tools-and-samples/policies/pages/cms_006713.aspx

Equal Employment Opportunity Commission (January 12, 1990). *Policy Guidance on Employer Liability under Title VII for Sexual Favoritism.* Retrieved September 10, 2020 from: https://www.eeoc.gov/laws/guidance/policy-guidance-employer-liability-under-title-vii-sexual-favoritism.

Farkas, Rachel, Johnson, Brittany, McMurray, Ryann, Schor, Noemi, and Smith, Allison (2019). State Regulation of Sexual Harassment. *Georgetown Journal of Gender & Law*, 20, 421-66.

Flores, Claudia (2019). Beyond the Bab Apple: Transforming the American Workplace for Women after #MeToo. *University of Chicago Law Review*, pp. 85-121.

Gallo, Amy (February 14, 2019). How to Approach an Office Romance (and How Not To). *Harvard Business Review*. Retrieved October 26, 2020 from: https//www.hbr.org/2019/02/how-to-approach-an-office-romance-and-how-not-to.

Garvin v. Southwestern Corr. LLC, 391 F. Supp. 3d 640, 2019 U.S. Dist. LEXIS 101421 (District Court for the Northern District Texas 2019).

Gasparino, Charles (September 20, 2020). Fink Looks Deep: BlackRock intrudes on office romances. *New York Post*, Post Business, p. 49.

Gilani, S.R.S., Cavico, F.J., and Mujtaba, B.G. (2014). Harassment in the Workplace: A Practical Review of the Laws in the United Kingdom and the United States. *Public Organization Review*, 14(1), 1-18.

Green, Michael Z. (2019). A New #MeToo Result: Rejecting Notions of Romantic Consent with Executives. *Employment Rights & Employment Policy Journal*, 23, 115-64.

Haigh, Emily and Wirtz, David M. (February 26, 2020). #MeToo: In Defense of Nondisclosure Agreements. *Lexology USA*. Retrieved 10/31/20 from: https://www.lexology.co/library/detail.aspx?g=21dob833-76dd-4030-a9cd.

Houseman, C. (Fall 2019). A# MeToo Moment: Third Circuit Gives Hope to Victims of Workplace Sexual Harassment. *Temple Law Review*, *92*, 205-296. Link: https://www.templelawreview.org/comment/a-metoo-moment-third-circuit-gives-hope-to-victims-of-workplace-sexual-harassment/

Huang, Mushu (2019). Legislative Responses to the Use of Non-Disclosure Agreements Regarding Sexual Misconduct Claims. *Seton Hall University eRepository*. Retrieved November 18, 2020 from: https://scholarship.shu.edu/student_scholarship/1023.

Kelly v. Howard I. Shapiro & Assocs. Consulting Eng'rs, P.C., 2012 U.S. Dist. LEXIS 110935 (District Court for the Eastern District of New York 2012).

Kieffer v. Tractor Supply Co., 2019 U.S. Dist. LEXIS 56523 (District Court for the District of 2019).

Kreis, Anthony Michael (2020). Defensive Glass Ceilings. *George Washington Law Review*, 147, pp. 147-202.

Leong, Nancy (2019). Them Too. *Washington University Law Review*, 96, 941-1006.

Levy, Kevin M. (May 21, 2019). Breaking the Silence: Good Riddance to Non-Disclosure Agreements in the #MeToo Era. *Rutgers Journal of Law & Public Policy*. Retrieved 10/31/20 from: rutgerspolicyjournal.org/breaking-silence-good-riddance-non-disclosure-agreements-MeToo-era.

Landler, Mark and Michael Barbaro (August 2, 2006). "Wal-Mart Finds that its Formula Doesn't Fit Every Culture". New York Times. Link: http://www.nytimes.com

Luthans, F. and Doh, J. (2021). *International Management: Culture, Strategy, and Behavior* (11th Ed.). McGraw-Hill: New York.

Marcus v. Leviton Mfg. Co., 2016 U.S. Dist. LEXIS 1065 (District Court for the Eastern District of New York 2016).

Mainiero, Lisa, and Jones, Kevin (2013a). Workplace Romance 2.0: Developing a Communication Ethics Model to Address Potential Sexual Harassment from Inappropriate Social Media Contacts Between Coworkers. *Journal of Business Ethics*, 114(2), 367-379.

Mainiero, Lisa, and Jones, Kevin (2013b). Sexual Harassment Versus Workplace Romance: Social Media Spillover and Textual Harassment in the Workplace. *Academy of Management Perspectives*, 27(3), 187-203.

McKissic v. City of Reno, 2019 U.S. Dist. LEXIS 119567 (District Court for the District of Nevada 2020).

Meritor Savings Bank v. Vinson, 477 U.S. 57 (1986).

Miller v. Aluminum Co. of America, 679 F. Supp. 495 (District Court for the Western District of Pennsylvania1988), *affirmed*, 856 F.2d 184 (Third Circuit Court of Appeals 1988.

Miller v. Dep't of Corr., 115 P.3d 77 (California Supreme Court 2005).

Morgan, Spencer (September 20-26, 2010). The End of the Office Affair. *Bloomberg Businessweek*, pp. 73-75.

Morris v. Acadian Ambulance Servs., 2015 U.S. Dist. LEXIS 43734 (District Court for the Eastern District of Louisiana 2015).

Mujtaba, B. G. (2022). Workforce Diversity Management: Inclusion and Equity Challenges, Competencies and Strategies *(3rd edition)*. ILEAD Academy: Florida.

Mujtaba, B. G., Cavico, F. J. (2020). Ethical Analysis of Office Romance and Sexual Favoritism Policies in the #MeToo Workplace and "Cancel Culture" Era. *SocioEconomic Challenges*, 4(4), 132-150.

Mujtaba, B.G., Cavico, F.J., and Senahip, T. (2020). Strategies for Personal, Organizational, and Professional Leadership Success. *Scientific Journal of Research and Reviews*, 2(3), 1-10.

Nichol v. City of Springfield, 2017 U.S. Dist. LEXIS 199467 (District Court for the District of Oregon 2017).

Noe, R. A., Hollenbeck, J. R., Gerhart, B., & Wright, P. M. (2021). *Human resource management: Gaining a competitive advantage* (12th ed.). McGraw-Hill: USA.

Pearce, II, John A. and Lipin, Ilya, A. (Summer 2015). Mitigating the Employer's Exposure to Third Party Claims for Hostile Work Environment. *Hastings Women's Law Journal*, 26, pp. 319-53.

Poff v. Oklahoma, 2017 U.S. App. LEXIS 5568 (Court of Appeals for the Tenth Circuit 2017).

Premack, D. (1965). Reinforcement theory. *Nebraska Symposium on motivation*, 13, 123-180.

Premack, D. (1961). Predicting instrumental performance from the independent rate of the contingent response. *Journal of Experimental Psychology*, 61, 163-171.

Premack, D. (1959). Toward empirical behavior laws: I. Positive reinforcement. *Psychological Review,* 66, 219-233.

Romero v. McCormick & Schmick Rest. Corp., 448 F. Supp. 3d 1(District Court for the District of Massachusetts 2020).

Safdar, Khadeeja (October 21, 2020). After #MeToo, Race Cases Fight NDAs. *Wall Street Journal*, pp. A1, A12.

Schneider v. GP Strategies Corp, 2017 U.S. Dist. LEXIS 17003 (District Court for the Eastern District of Kentucky 2017).

Shellenbarger, Sue (February 10, 2010). For Office Romance, the Secret's Out. *The Wall Street Journal*, pp. D1, D2.

Smith-Lee, Emily (2020). Sexual Harassment and Nondisclosure Agreements. *Sinlaw.com*. Retrieved 10/31/20 from: sinlaw.com/sexual-harassment-and-non-disclosure-agreements.html.

Spiggle Law Firm. *Protecting Workers from Wrongful Employment Practices*. Nondisclosure Agreements: What Are They, and How Do They Work in Sexual Harassment Cases. Retrieved 10/31/20 from: spigglelaw.com/employment-blog/non-disclosure-agreements-work-sexual-harassment-cases.

Srinivasan, Ama (February 2020). Sex as a Pedagogical Failure. *Yale Law Journal*, pp. 1100-1146.

Stewart v. SBE Entm't Grp., LLC, 239 F. Supp. 3d 1235 (District Court for the District of Nevada 2017).

Taylor & Ring (April 20, 2020). If You Have Signed an NDA, Can You Report a Sexual Assault. *Taylor & Ring Blog*. Retrieved 10/31/20 from: tayorring.com/blog/if-you-have-signed-an-NDA-can-you-report-a-sexual-assault.

Tippett, Elizabeth (Winter 2019). Non-Disclosure Agreements and the #MeToo Movement. *Dispute Resolution Magazine*. Retrieved 10/31/20 from: americanbar.org/groups/dispute-resolution/publication/dispute-resolution-magazine/2019/winter-2019.

Trottman, Melanie (January 12, 2011). Charges of Bias at Work Increase. *The Wall Street Journal*, p. A2.

U.S. Equal Employment Opportunity Commission (1990). Policy Guidance on Employer Liability under Title VII for Sexual Favoritism. Retrieved from: https://www.eeoc.gov/laws/guidance/policy-guidance-employer-liability-under-title-vii-sexual-favoritism

Vault Careers (February 11, 2018). The 2018 Vault Office Romance Survey Results. Link: https://www.vault.com/blogs/workplace-issues/2018-vault-office-romance-survey-results

Vault.com's. (2010). Office romance survey. Retrieved from: http://www.vault.com/officeromancesurvey

Wasche v. Orchard Hosp., 2020 U.S. Dist. LEXIS 152286 (District Court for the Eastern District of California 2020).

Weiss, Deborah M. (2019). Sexual Harms without Misogyny. *University of Chicago Legal Forum*, pp. 299-341.

Wilkie, D. (2013). Forbidden Love: Workplace-Romance Policies Now Stricter. SHRM. Retrieved from: https://www.shrm.org/resourcesandtools/hr-topics/employee-relations/pages/forbidden-love-workplace-romance-policies-stricter.aspx

Workable.com (2020). *Employee relationships in the workplace policy.* Retrieved October 5, 2020 from: www.resources.workable.com/workplace-policy-romance-policy-example.

Yuldashev, O. and Yusupov, N. (2016). Workplace Romance. Lexology. Retrieved from: https://www.lexology.com/library/detail.aspx?g=13454c88-77cf-4def-92d2-325c05d3047a

Zillman, Claire (July 18, 2018). Employers are clamping down of office romance in the #MeToo movement, but it will never die. *Fortune.* Retrieved October 28, 2020, from: https://fortune.com/2018/07/18/metoo-office-romance-workplace-policy.

Zajonc, R. B. (1968). Attitudinal effects of mere exposure. *Journal of Personality and Social Psychology, 9*(2), 1–27.

Author Biographies

Bahaudin G. Mujtaba is Professor of Human Resources, International Management, and Organizational Behavior at Nova Southeastern University's H. Wayne Huizenga College of Business and Entrepreneurship in Fort Lauderdale, Florida, United States of America. Bahaudin was awarded the prestigious annual "*Faculty of the Year Award.*" Internationally, Bahaudin received the "Pride of HR Profession" Award at the World HRD Congress annual conference, held in Mumbai, India. Bahaudin served as a corporate manager, trainer and management development specialist and consultant in the retail industry for sixteen years. Bahaudin is SHRM-SCP - certified by the Society of Human Resource Management as a Senior Certified Professional (SHRM-SCP). He is also a certified "Diversity" and "Situational Leadership" trainer. Bahaudin has lectured in or served as a speaker for national and international conferences around the globe, including in Thailand, Vietnam, Japan, China, India, Pakistan, Afghanistan, Morocco, Bahama, Brazil, Jamaica, Malaysia, and others. Bahaudin has written and published over one hundred peer reviewed journal articles, and he has authored and co-authored twenty books. Bahaudin was born in Khoshie of Logar and raised in Kabul, Afghanistan. He finished Fort Myers High School, then attended Edison Community College, University of Central Florida, Nova University, and Nova Southeastern University to achieve his academic dreams. Email: mujtaba@nova.edu.

Frank J. Cavico is a Professor of Law, Business Law, and Business Ethics. He has taught for over 40 years at the law school, university, and college level, most recently in the undergraduate business and MBA programs at the H. Wayne Huizenga College of Business and Entrepreneurship of Nova Southeastern University in Ft. Lauderdale, Florida, where he recently retired as a Professor Emeritus after 30 years of service, though he is still teaching at Nova Southeastern University as an adjunct professor. He came to Nova Southeastern University to develop a graduate law and ethics course for the Huizenga College's MBA program. He holds a B.A degree in political science from Gettysburg College, a M.A. in political science from Drew University in Madison, N.J., a J.D. from St. Mary's University School of Law in San Antonio, Texas, as well as an LL.M in Torts and Product Liability from the University of San Diego School of Law. He is the recipient of several teaching honors and awards; and he is the author of several books and numerous law review and management journal articles. He resides in Lauderdale by the Sea, Florida, with his wife, Nancy, a registered nurse.

10

Index